The GLORY OF THE GREEN

The Celtic Trophies

JOHN TRAYNOR   DOUGLAS RUSSELL

THE GLORY OF THE GREEN, The Celtic Trophies was written and compiled by John Traynor and Douglas Russell.

First published 1991 by Holmes McDougall Publishing & Print Limited

© 1991

All rights reserved. No part of this publication may be reproduced, stored in a retrieval system or transmitted in any form or by any means electronic, electrostatic, mechanical, photocopying, magnetic tape, recording or otherwise without the prior permission of the publishers.

British Library Cataloguing-in-Publication Data

Traynor, John, *1947-*
   The glory of the green : the Celtic trophies.
   I. Title II. Russell, Douglas, *1948-*
796.334630941443

ISBN 0715728504
ISBN 0715728482 pbk

Photography by Michael Siebert, Edinburgh
Typesetting and Page Make-up by Trinity Typesetting, Edinburgh
Origination by Centre Graphics, Livingston

Printed in Scotland by Holmes McDougall Publishing & Print Limited

The GLORY OF THE GREEN
The Celtic Trophies

CONTENTS

4	FOREWORD	ATHLETICS/CYCLING	60
6	INTRODUCTION	CENTENARY CUP	62
9	CORRIDOR CABINETS (COLOUR)	REAL MADRID SILVER CABIN	64
10	MAIN TROPHY CABINET (COLOUR)	SCOTTISH LEAGUE PLAQUE	66
12	CORONATION CUP (COLOUR)	TEAM POOL PLATE	67
14	ROSENBORG LONGBOAT	VICTORY IN EUROPE CUP	68
17	WORLD OF SOCCER CUP	FERENCVAROS VASE (COLOUR)	71
18	D.V.T.K. VASE	GLASGOW CUP (COLOUR)	72
20	RED STAR PLAQUE	STATUE OF SAMOTHRACE	74
22	MOSTAR PLAQUE	U.S. TOURS/INDIAN CHIEF	76
24	B.B.C. AWARDS	U.S. TOURS/TOUR ARCHIVE	78
26	VINTAGE FOOTBALLS	EMPIRE EXHIBITION TROPHY (COLOUR)	81
27	MANCHESTER UNITED	FEYENOORD CLOCK (COLOUR)	82
29	EUROPEAN CUP REPLICA (COLOUR)	JOHN GLASS PORTRAIT (COLOUR)	83
30	CELTIC PARK FOYER (COLOUR)	THE CAMPAIGN PENNANTS (COLOUR)	84
32	JERSEY CABINET (COLOUR)	ISRAELI VASE (COLOUR)	85
34	JOCK STEIN PORTRAIT (COLOUR)	FEYENOORD JUG (COLOUR)	86
36	VIAREGGIO TROPHY	JOHN THOMSON CABINET (COLOUR)	87
39	CUP OF CHAMPIONS	LEAGUE SHIELD (COLOUR)	88
40	ATLETICO MADRID BUST	SCHOONER VALDIVIA	90
42	TIMISOARA VASE	FLEMISH WARRIOR	93
45	DUBAI CHALLENGE CUP	BENFICA EAGLE	94
46	PATSY GALLACHER PORTRAIT	GREEK GIFTS	96
49	POLAR BEAR TROPHY	REAL MADRID GOLDEN BALL	99
51	ST MUNGO CUP (COLOUR)	VINTAGE MEDALS	101
52	R.M.S. CELTIC (COLOUR)	CHARLIE TULLY CABINET	102
53	BOAVISTA CARAVEL (COLOUR)	CENTENARY GIFTS	104
54	GLASGOW EXHIBITION CUP (COLOUR)	JOHNNY CRUM'S JERSEY	106
57	CITY OF GLASGOW PLAQUE	KRAKOW VASE	108
59	VALENCIA TROPHY	BROTHER WALFRID BOWL	110
	ACKNOWLEDGEMENTS 112		

FOREWORD

Celtic Football Club is a unique football club. It is unique for the loyalty of its support, for its worldwide charismatic reputation and for its achievements on the football field. Many of those achievements are remembered and commemorated through the trophies and memorabilia that can be found at Celtic Park. Of the hundreds of cups, plates, trophies and many other mementoes, some sixty of the most significant are to be found in the pages of this book. For visitors to the Club, guided tours are available and the trophies on display bring to life the memorable history of a great football club.

On display is an exact replica of the European Cup won by Celtic in 1967, the first ever British club to win this trophy. Also on view is the trophy which commemorates the winning of six League Championships in a row, a trophy of unusual and attractive design. Another trophy on display of particular note is The Coronation Cup. These are just three of the trophies to be found in this book which help to illustrate some of the tremendous achievements of Celtic teams.

We hope that this book gives not only an insight into Celtic Football Club but also gives pleasure to football supporters irrespective of their chosen team. We would also like to think that as many people as possible can come to Celtic Park and enjoy the trophies on view and the atmosphere generated throughout Celtic Football Club.

Kevin Kelly
Chairman
Celtic Football Club

INTRODUCTION

The Celtic Football Club is more than just another sporting institution — for generations of supporters throughout the world it has been and *is* a way of life. Indeed, there are those for whom life itself would be almost unimaginable without Celtic as its focal point.

And yet there are many thousands of such fans who, while well aware of the club's glorious heritage and proud competitive record, have never been privileged to pass through the hallowed portals of Celtic Park to witness the dazzling array of trophies and memorabilia, amassed over more than a century, which is distributed throughout the stadium complex. More than anything, this book is for *them*.

The history of The Celtic Football Club has been copiously and eloquently recorded in many volumes. Various Celtic luminaries and a string of eminent club historians have, each in their own distinctive style and from their own peculiar standpoint, charted the team's progress from its origins as a local charitable trust and source of revenue for co-founder Brother Walfrid's *'Poor Children's Dinner Table'* up to the particular stage of its development at which they were writing.

This being so, it is well-nigh impossible to bring anything genuinely fresh to bear on the telling of the Celtic story, nor *is* it the purpose of this book to amplify or expand upon the respective historians' work. While, inevitably, this text will overlap and interweave with much of what has been written hitherto, the principal intention is simply to catalogue and 'showcase' the Celtic collection for posterity and for the sheer pleasure of anyone who has Celtic in his blood.

From the moment you cross the threshold of Celtic Park into the airy foyer, you sense that this is a *special* place. More than a stadium, it is a virtual shrine to the hundreds of young men who have graced the hoops (or the forerunners of that most distinctive garb, introduced in season 1903/04) since the pioneering days of the late 1880s. Somehow the aura of the great ones, who remain forever young in the minds and hearts of Celtic folk, still pervades the complex . . . Kelly . . . Quinn . . . Gallacher . . . McGrory . . . Thomson . . . Tully . . . Johnstone . . . Dalglish . . . and around every corner a fresh delight lies in wait to surprise and enchant you.

The heart of the collection is in the Board Room, whose spectacular spotlit display cabinets house, amongst many others, the epic trophies, those 'one-off' prizes in which Celtic have specialised over the years and which are held in such reverential awe by supporters:

The Glasgow Exhibition Trophy (1902) . . . The Empire Exhibition Trophy (1938) . . . The Victory in Europe Cup (1945) . . . The St Mungo Cup (1951) . . . The Coronation Cup (1953).

Also on permanent display in the Board Room are The European Champions' Cup replica (1967), The League Shield (1904/05 - 1909/10) and The City of Glasgow Commemorative Plaque (season 1966/67). Many will also be surprised and delighted by the beauty of The Ferencvaros Vase and its intriguing story.

In the old main corridor, off the Board Room, you will find The John Thomson Memorial Cabinet, installed in honour of that legendary 'Prince of Goalkeepers', who quite literally died for the jersey at the very height of his considerable powers. This particular exhibit has become almost a place of pilgrimage for the many visitors to Celtic Park, such is Thomson's stature in Celtic folklore.

Mounting the staircase from the foyer you will pass The Tully Cabinet, dedicated to the incomparable Irishman who did so much to drag Celtic out of the doldrums in the late 1940s and early '50s — 'Cheeky Charlie', who had a hand in so many famous Celtic triumphs, none moreso than the legendary '7-1' League Cup Final against Rangers in 1957. Here also hang the painting of the *R.M.S. Celtic,* whose fascinating story is not widely known, even in the most intimate Celtic circles and the portrait of John Glass, the indefatigable founder member of the club and its first President (effectively, Chairman). This principal though largely unsung hero of the Celtic saga is featured inside.

Other principal locations of the kaleidoscopic collection which constitutes *'The Celtic Trophies'* are the stadium's various corridors and landings; the Stein Lounge, with its imposing portrait of 'The Big Man'; the Celtic Suite; the Europa Suite; and the Lisbon Suite, which houses the 1967 European Cup Pennant Cabinet.

Of course, no mere book could possibly rival an actual visit to the Parkhead trophy complex but we are confident that through these pages you will sense the unique atmosphere which is essentially Celtic.

So if *your* blood stirs to the strains of 'The Celtic Song', relax awhile and absorb 'THE GLORY OF THE GREEN'.

Corridor Cabinets featuring Jock Stein, Jimmy McGrory and Pennants from the 1969/70 European Cup campaign.

Main Trophy Cabinet in Board Room.

THE CORONATION CUP
1953

Celtic F.C. has a proud tradition of success in special 'one-off' competitions in which the prize becomes the outright property of the winner. No matter the team's prevailing form, such special circumstances seem to bring out the best in the club, as the Coronation Cup of 1953 bears witness.

The competition featured the top clubs of the time from Scotland and England. To be honest, Celtic's inclusion was probably more a reflection of the team's reputation and crowd-pulling potential than its relative standing at the time. Nonetheless, the unlikely events of that summer were destined to weave their way into Celtic folklore and become immortalised in one of the more imaginative club anthems.

Remarkably, had it not been for the stubborn determination of the Chairman of the day, Bob Kelly (later, Sir Robert) in facing down a player rebellion over terms for the tournament, Celtic might not even have taken part. What a gap that would have left in the trophy cabinet!

When battle commenced, the 'Bhoys' surprised everyone by toppling the mighty Arsenal 1-0. As if that wasn't enough they went on to dispose of Manchester United (earlier conquerors of 'Old Firm' rivals, Rangers) by 2-1, to set up an unlikely all-Scottish final against Hibernian.

Final day was May 30th . . . 'and, oh, what a scene — the terracings were covered in banners of green!'

Celtic took the lead in twenty-eight minutes, courtesy of a typical long-range shot by Neil Mochan, set up by a pass from the gifted Willie Fernie. Hibs could not penetrate a defence brilliantly marshalled by Jock Stein and Bobby Evans and bolstered by an inspired goalkeeper in Johnny Bonnar.

Three minutes from time an Evans interception and pass sparked the move which ended in a second, decisive strike by Walsh. Another memorable chapter had been written in the magical history of The Celtic Football Club!

The team in the final was: Bonnar; Haughney, Rollo; Evans, Stein, McPhail; Collins, Walsh, Mochan, Peacock, Fernie.

The only change in the line-up throughout the competition was the introduction of Fernie for the final in place of the injured Charlie Tully.

Height: 21"

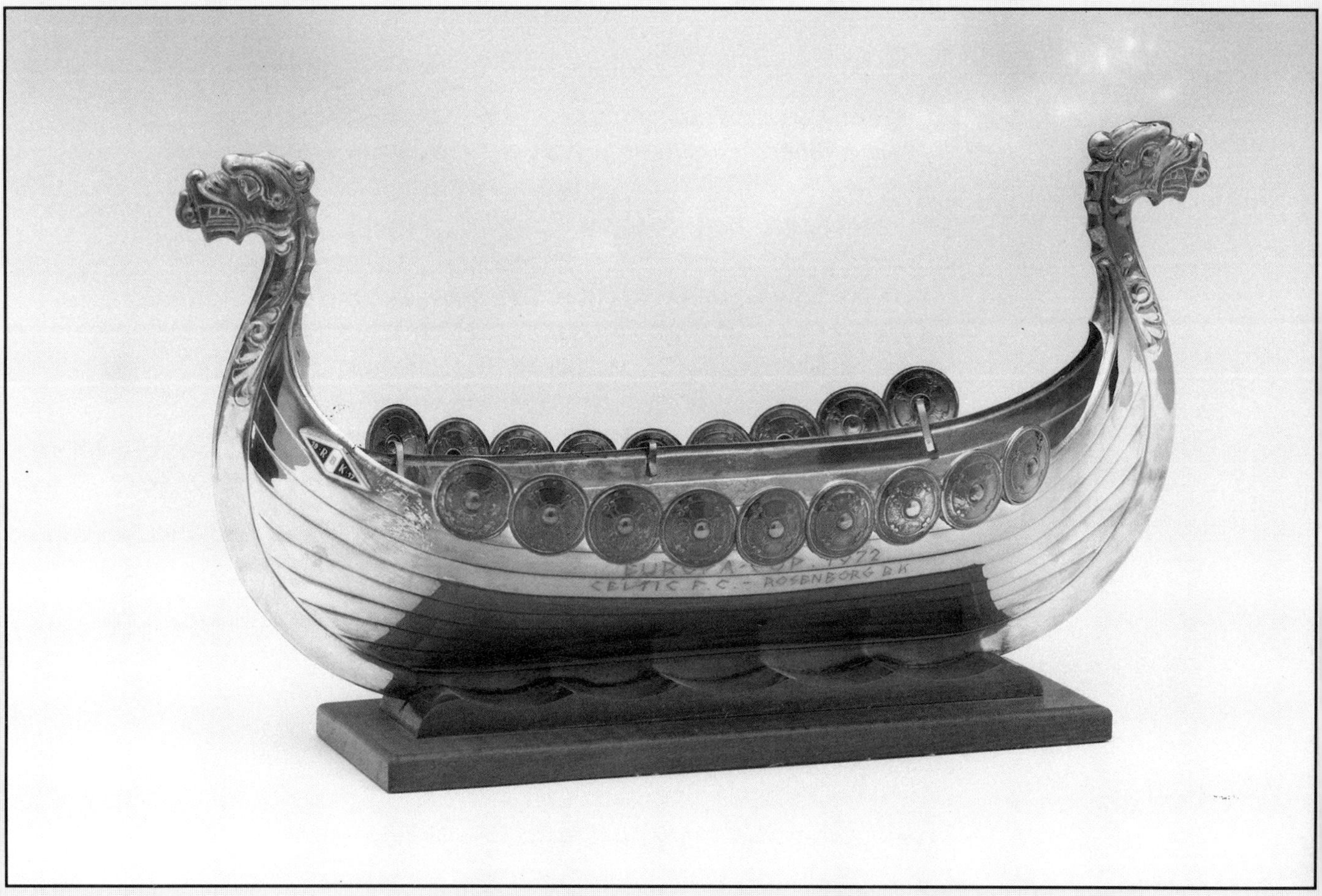

THE CELTIC FOOTBALL & ATHLETIC COY LTD
1888

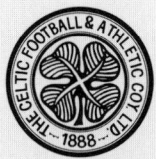

ROSENBORG LONGBOAT
1972

The silver replica of a Viking longboat was the gift of Norwegian champions Rosenborg Trondheim in the European Cup first round of season 1972/73.

Despite almost total domination of the first leg in Glasgow, a match played at Hampden Park on account of renovation work at Parkhead, Celtic only managed two goals and carelessly conceded one in a rare Rosenborg breakaway four minutes into the second half.

An alarming lethargy saw Celtic 1-0 down at the interval in the second leg in Trondheim. Fortunately, or more likely after a few choice words from Jock Stein in the dressing room, they woke up to carry the game to Rosenborg with a vengeance in the second half. Macari and Hood restored some sanity to the scoreline before Kenny Dalglish wrapped things up nicely from a glorious Johnstone pass which capped a scintillating run the whole length of the pitch.

Celtic won 5-2 on aggregate. Rosenborg goalkeeper, Geir Karlsen was later signed but failed to make an impact and moved on to a spell with Dunfermline Athletic.

September 13th: **First Leg** Celtic 2 Rosenborg 1
Macari (17)
Deans (44)

Celtic: Williams; McGrain, Callaghan; Murdoch, McNeill, Connelly; Hood, Dalglish, Deans, Macari, Wilson (Lennox).

September 27th: **Second Leg** Rosenborg 1 Celtic 3
Macari (56)
Hood (82)
Dalglish (89)

Celtic: Williams; McGrain, McCluskey; Murdoch, McNeill, Connelly; Johnstone, Dalglish, Macari, Hood, Callaghan.

Length: 14"

WORLD OF SOCCER CUP
1977

In the summer of 1977 Celtic undertook a tour of Australia and the Far East. It was the club's longest ever tour in terms of distance and the hope was that the spirit of 1966 could be rekindled. Unfortunately, something of a damper was put on proceedings by the withdrawal and apparent restlessness of Kenny Dalglish, who was on the threshold of his departure to Liverpool.

Nevertheless, the tour did produce this impressive trophy, won in four-way competition against Arsenal, the Australian national eleven and old rivals, Red Star Belgrade, whom Celtic beat in the final in Melbourne.

July 31st: Final   Celtic 2   Red Star Belgrade 0

Height: 21½"

D.V.T.K. VASE
1980

This attractive piece of porcelain is a reminder of the 7-2 aggregate victory over Diosgyeori Miskolc of Hungary in the first round of the 1980/81 European Cup Winners' Cup.

The decisive first leg at Celtic Park was the classic 'game of two halves'. After a luckless (and goalless) first forty-five minutes, Celtic went on a spree after the interval, snatching six goals in a devastating twenty-seven minute spell, including a Frank McGarvey hat-trick.

August 20th: **First Leg**   Celtic 6   Diosgyeori 0
McGarvey (52, 65, 70)
McCluskey (59, 79)
Sullivan (71)

Celtic: Bonner; Sneddon, McGrain; Aitken, McAdam, MacLeod (Doyle); Provan (Nicholas), Sullivan, McGarvey, Burns, McCluskey.

September 3rd: **Second Leg**   Diosgyeori 2   Celtic 1
Nicholas (24)

Celtic: Bonner; Sneddon, McGrain; Aitken, McAdam, MacLeod; Provan, Sullivan, McGarvey, Burns, Nicholas.

Height: 14½"

RED STAR PLAQUE
1968

One of Celtic's most memorable European nights is recalled by this carved wooden plaque, a memento of the second round tie against the Yugoslav champions in the European Cup of 1968/69. A heaving crowd at Celtic Park for the first leg witnessed a virtual two-man demolition job as Bobby Murdoch and Jimmy Johnstone tore the heart out of the well-fancied Red Star in a pulsating second half.

Legend has it that the wily Jock Stein, conscious of 'Jinky's' fear of flying, promised the mercurial winger that he need not travel for the second leg if the tie was 'won' at home. Johnstone's response was devastating. Prompted by the majestic Murdoch, he ran amok, grabbing two himself for good measure, including the last and most spectacular goal of the night, lashing the ball into the net after a typically mazy run nine minutes from time.

Celtic won the tie 6-2 on aggregate.

November 13th: **First Leg**   Celtic 5   Red Star Belgrade 1
Murdoch (3)
Johnstone (47, 81)
Lennox (50)
Wallace (75)

Celtic: Fallon; Craig, Gemmell; Murdoch, McNeill, Brogan; Johnstone, Wallace, Chalmers, Lennox, Hughes.

November 27th: **Second Leg**   Red Star Belgrade 1   Celtic 1
Wallace (76)

Celtic: Fallon; Craig, Gemmell; Brogan, McNeill, Clark; Connelly, Lennox, Chalmers (Wallace), Murdoch, Hughes.

Diameter: 14½"

MOSTAR PLAQUE
1989

Celtic were drawn against the other Belgrade club, Partizan, in the European Cup Winners' Cup of 1989/90. A U.E.F.A. ruling following crowd trouble in Belgrade the previous season meant that the Yugoslav leg was played in Mostar.

The commemorative plaque from that match depicts the famous bridge from which locals have traditionally made a perilous leap into the fast-flowing river far below as a somewhat dubious tourist attraction.

The tie ended 6-6 on aggregate but Celtic lost out on the 'away goals' rule despite winning 5-4 at Celtic Park, a match which featured a stunning four-goal performance from close-season signing Dariusz 'Jacki' Dziekanowski.

Diameter: 12½"

B.B.C. AWARDS

Team of the Year Trophy
1967

Not surprisingly, the all-conquering Celtic side of season 1966/67 walked away with the prestigious 'Sportsview' team award for that year. This was the forerunner of the present-day team section of the B.B.C. Television Sports Review of the Year presentations.

Height: 8½"

Quizball Trophies
1969/70

The popular 'Quizball' programme of the late 'sixties was a predecessor of today's 'Question of Sport'. These trophies were won on that series by teams representing the club, including former captain and manager, Billy McNeill, with actor John Cairney as a celebrity guest.

Height: 8½"

VINTAGE FOOTBALLS

These exhibits illustrate the type of ball used in senior professional football in the 'thirties, 'forties and 'fifties. Just like the game itself in that earlier era, they are very different from the lightweight, waterproof balls with which the modern player and fan have become so familiar. Present-day juggling, swerving and spectacular shooting might not have been so commonplace without major advances in equipment from those soggy days of dubbin and laces.

The ball on the left is the actual ball used in the historic Exhibition Cup Final at Ibrox Stadium in 1938 (see page 80). It bears the autographs of the winning Celtic players and legendary manager William Maley as well as those of other players over the years.

MANCHESTER UNITED

Red Devil
Bobby Charlton testimonial
1972

September 18th: Manchester United 0   Celtic 0

Height: 13"

Glass Ball
Danny McGrain testimonial
1980

August 4th: Celtic 0   Manchester United 0

Height: 9"

THE EUROPEAN CHAMPIONS' CUP
Replica

On May 25th 1967, in Lisbon's National Stadium, Celtic became not only the first Scottish but also the first British and indeed, the first non-Latin club to win Europe's premier trophy (see page 84, 'The Campaign', for details).

In an exhilarating march to the final, arguably the most exciting team ever to grace the green and white hoops disposed of Swiss champions Zurich, Nantes of France, Vojvodina Novi Sad, champions of Yugoslavia and Czechoslovakia's Dukla Prague. The formidable Czechs were led by the great Josef Masopust, who had inspired his country to the World Cup Final of 1962.

The second leg of the quarter-final tie with Vojvodina must go down as one of the most tense and pulsating nights ever at Celtic Park.

In the final, the opposition could scarcely have been more formidable — twice former champions, Internazionale of Milan. With their exalted status, the Italian superstars may have felt the match would be something of a formality. Celtic, however, under the shrewd guidance of Jock Stein, scored all the pre-match psychological points, culminating in an incident during the long walk to the pitch. Imagine Inter's perplexity when the unpretentious Scots broke into a chorus of 'The Celtic Song'!

The rest is history, with Celtic storming back from a seventh minute penalty reverse to gradually wear down the negative men from Milan. The equalizer came from a typical Tommy Gemmell rocket in the sixty-third minute and Steve Chalmers wrong-footed goalkeeper Sarti with his deflection of a Murdoch shot five minutes from time for the historic winner.

An especially pleasing aspect of the victory was the fact that the Celtic team were all Scottish born, the first time the trophy had been won by a team of home nationals.

The accolades came thick and fast, perhaps the most telling comment coming, not for the first time, from the inimitable Bill Shankly, who drew Jock Stein aside to tell him, 'John, you are now immortal.'

The victorious Celtic team was: Simpson; Craig, Gemmell; Murdoch, McNeill, Clark; Johnstone, Wallace, Chalmers, Auld, Lennox.

Height: 31½"

Foyer prior to mid-year modifications, 1991

European Opponents' Jerseys.

JOHN 'JOCK' STEIN C.B.E. 1922-1985

Player/Captain 1951-1956:
*Coronation Cup 1953
League & Cup 'double' 1953/54
Glasgow Cup 1955/56*

Manager 1965-1975/1976-1978:
*League Championships 10
Scottish Cups 8   League Cups 6
Glasgow Cups 4
European Cup 1*

Mr Stein missed the whole of season 1975/76 due to severe injuries sustained in a car crash on the A74 while returning from holiday, July 1975. Sean Fallon stood in during his absence.

JOCK STEIN

In any appraisal of major figures in the history of Celtic, the name of Jock Stein is sure to figure prominently. As player, coach and manager, his collective contribution was matched by very few, if any, before him and none since.

Plucked from the obscurity of Welsh non-League football in December 1951, Stein inherited the captaincy (at first temporarily and then outright) from Sean Fallon following the Irishman's unfortunate double break of an arm against Falkirk just before Christmas 1952. In that role he went on to lead the club to one of its greatest triumphs in the Coronation Cup the following May and to the League and Cup 'double' of 1953/54. In so doing he first began to reveal the qualities of leadership and organisation which he would later exercise to such devastating effect in management.

Quite simply, both on the field and in the manager's chair, Jock Stein was, for Celtic, the right man at the right time.

It is often forgotten that some of the key figures among the heroes of Lisbon had come under Jock's shrewd guidance in their formative years.

As youth coach in the late 'fifties, he helped nurture several of the youngsters he would later 'inherit' as the 'Kelly Kids' on his return to Celtic Park after cutting his managerial teeth at Dunfermline and Hibernian. Sharp teeth they were, too, as Celtic discovered in the 1961 Scottish Cup Final, going down 2-0 to a Dunfermline Athletic then under 'The Big Man's' influence.

It is now part of Celtic folklore that Jock Stein masterminded the historic 'nine-in-a-row' run of League Championships. It is less common knowledge that each of those titles was wrapped up on a different Scottish ground — and none at Celtic Park! The only 'home' clincher (1970/71) had to be switched to Hampden on account of reconstruction work at Parkhead.

Jock's portrait now dominates The Stein Lounge, the suite within the Celtic Park complex dedicated to his memory.

VIAREGGIO TROPHY
1988

Celtic were presented with this splendid trophy to commemorate their participation in a prestigious close-season tournament following the 'double' triumph of the Centenary season of 1987/88. The high-powered opposition were the newly-crowned European Champions, Porto of Portugal, Cup Winners' Cup holders Mechelen of Belgium and runners-up Ajax of Holland.

Not surprisingly, Celtic struggled a bit in such exalted company but gave a good account of themselves, only losing narrowly to a late goal by Porto in their semi-final.

Height: 20"

CUP OF CHAMPIONS
1968

Season 1967/68 had been a difficult one for Celtic. Hardly surprising, following as it did the sensational golden year which reached its climax in the Lisbon European Cup triumph.

Nevertheless, three of the previous year's five trophies were retained, including the vital League Championship and so, when they set off in the close season for a tour of the United States, Canada and South America, it was still as proud Scottish champions.

On that tour, the reigning Italian champions, A.C. Milan, were confronted twice. The first meeting resulted in a creditable 1-1 draw against the newly-crowned winners of the European Cup Winners' Cup. It was the second encounter, however, which produced this impressively-mounted trophy.

The match took place on June 1st 1968 in the Canadian National Exhibition Stadium in Toronto. Celtic won decisively 2-0, with goals from Bobby Lennox and the ever-reliable Charlie Gallagher, who had so long and faithfully performed the role of 'utility man' in the shadow of those who were to become 'Lisbon Lions' but who had come into his own in clinching the 1967/68 championship during the prolonged absence of Bertie Auld.

Height: 32"

CUP OF CHAMPIONS

GLASGOW CELTIC - VS - A.C. MILAN
JUNE 1, 1968
CANADIAN NATIONAL EXHIBITION STADIUM
TORONTO, CANADA
PRESENTED BY
TORONTO CITY SOCCER CLUB

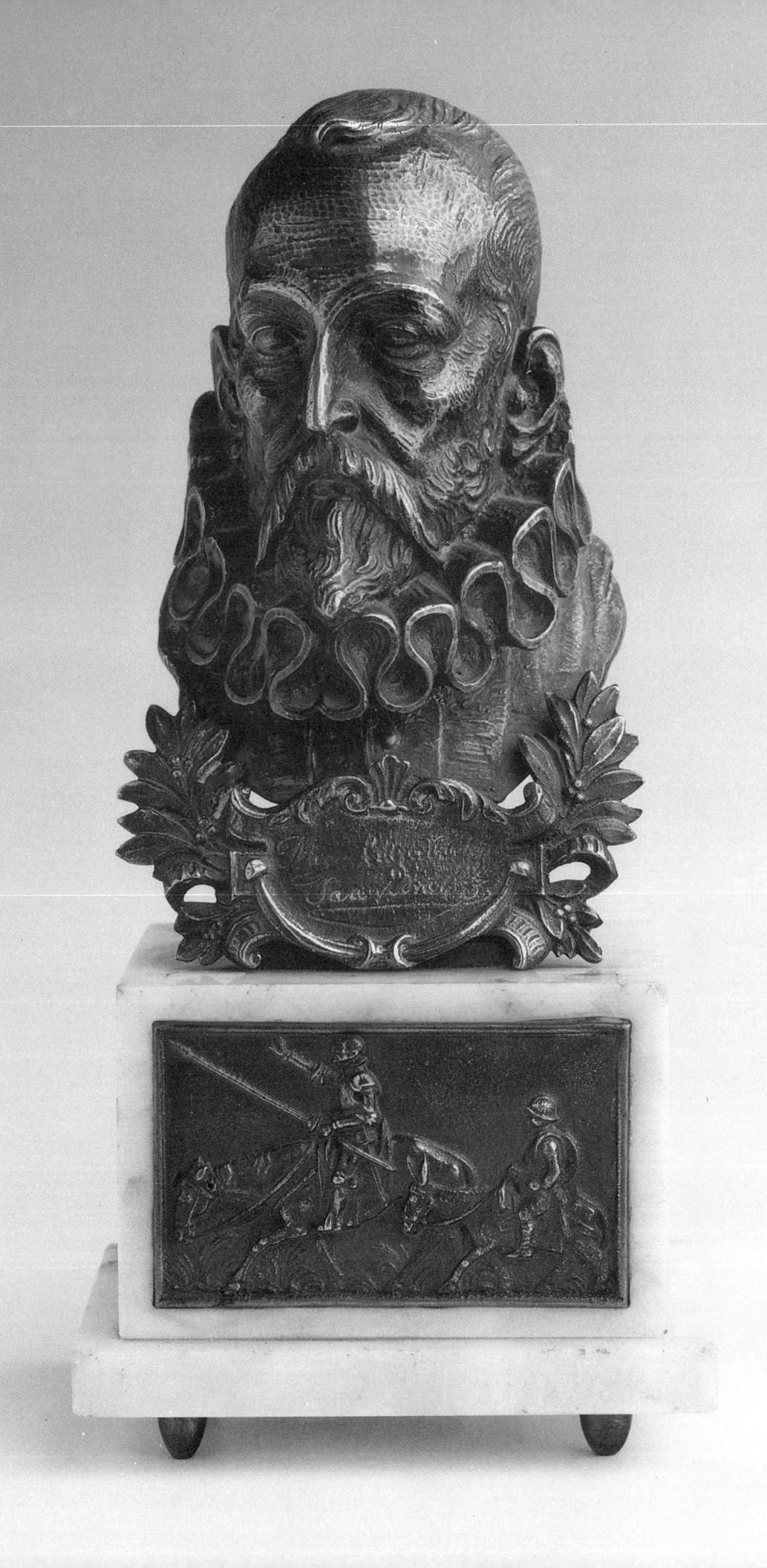

ATLETICO MADRID BUST
1974

Handsome though this bust of a Spanish aristocrat may be, it holds nothing but bitter memories of an infamous European Cup semi-final from season 1973/74.

Having disposed of Turku (Finland), Vejle (Denmark) and Basle (Switzerland) to reach the last four of the competition, Celtic were drawn against Atletico Madrid, who were desperate to emulate some of the success of their more illustrious neighbours. Sadly, under the direction of the notorious Juan Carlos Lorenzo, they were none too particular about their methods, which led to a most cynical first leg display at Celtic Park.

The Spaniards wildly celebrated the 0-0 scoreline, secured in a vicious, intimidating manner which cost them three orderings-off and seven bookings. Despite six U.E.F.A. suspensions for such shocking conduct, Atletico sealed the tie on a 2-0 aggregate with a couple of late goals in Madrid.

Mercifully, the Spanish hard men got their come-uppance in the final, where they were dispatched 4-0 by a Bayern Munich side on its way to three successive Champions' Cup victories.

April 10th: **First Leg** Celtic 0 Atletico Madrid 0

Celtic: Connaghan; Hay, Brogan; Murray, McNeill, McCluskey; Johnstone, Hood, Deans (Wilson), Callaghan, Dalglish.

April 24th: **Second Leg** Atletico Madrid 2 Celtic 0

Celtic: Connaghan; McGrain, Brogan; Hay, McNeill, McCluskey; Johnstone, Murray, Dalglish, Hood, Lennox.

Height: 12½"

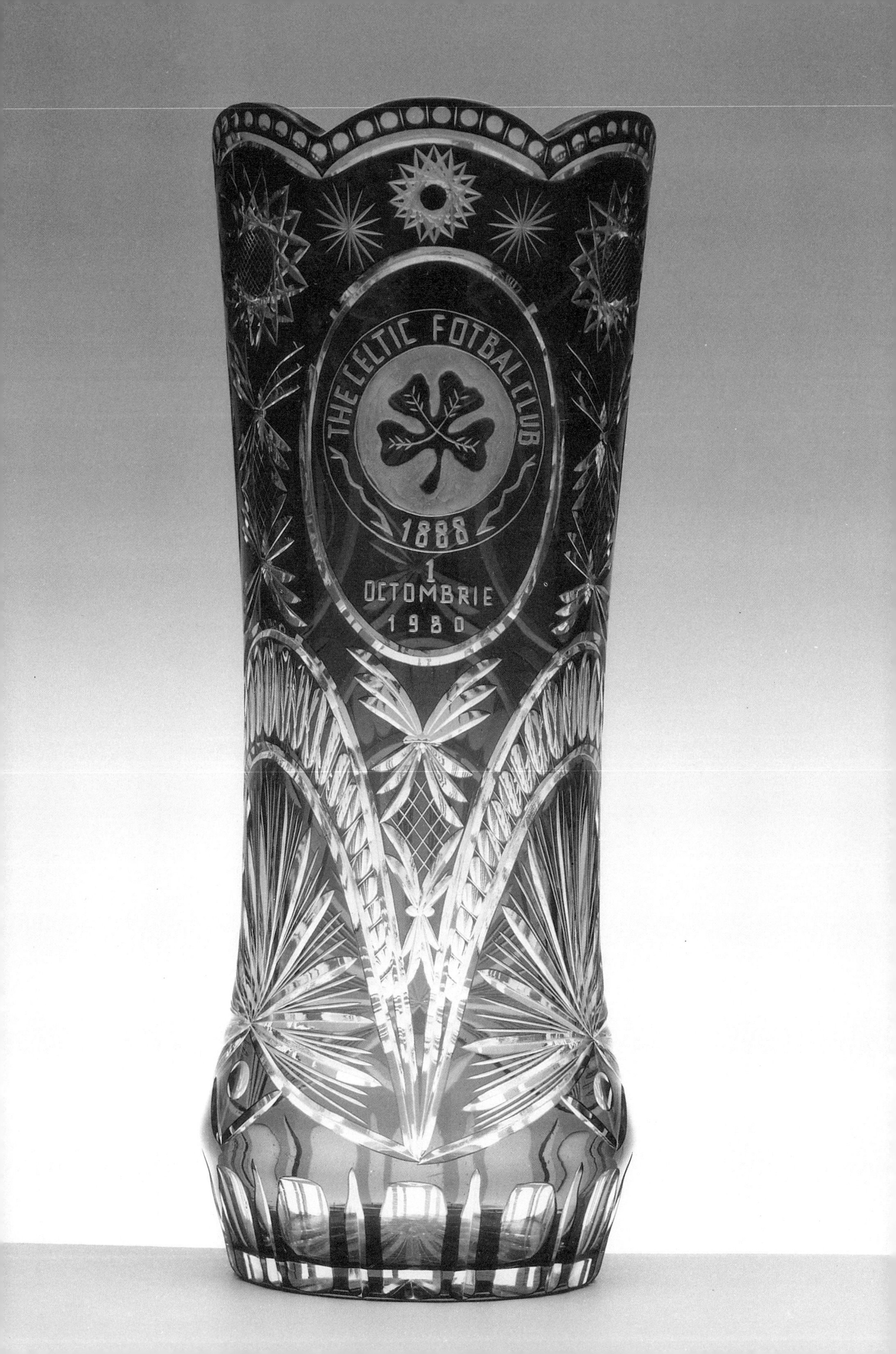
THE CELTIC FOTBAL CLUB
1888
1
OCTOMBRIE
1980

TIMISOARA VASE
1980

This stunning blue vase is a grim reminder of the European Cup Winners' Cup second round tie against Politechnica Timisoara of Romania in season 1980/81.

The tie should really have been made safe in the first leg at Celtic Park, in which Celtic scorned opportunities, suffered some bad luck and eventually conceded a decisive goal. In the event, a hazardous away leg was left in prospect.

The controversial return was decided by a scrappy goal following a goalmouth collision after Latchford had clutched a cross from the right. Again, Celtic had had perhaps the best of the exchange overall but were hampered by the early dismissal of centre-half Roddie MacDonald in a questionable double ordering-off incident with his Romanian opposite number.

September 17th: **First Leg**   Celtic 2   Politechnica Timisoara 1
Nicholas (19, 42)

Celtic: Bonner; Sneddon, McGrain; Aitken, McAdam, MacLeod (Conroy); Provan (Doyle), Sullivan, McCluskey, Burns, Nicholas.

October 1st: **Second Leg**   Politechnica Timisoara 1   Celtic 0

Celtic: Latchford; Sneddon, McAdam, MacDonald, McGrain; Sullivan, Aitken, MacLeod; McGarvey, Nicholas, Provan.

Aggregate score 2-2 (Politechnica Timisoara won on 'away goals' rule).

Height: 18½"

DUBAI CHALLENGE CUP
1989

Celtic qualified twice in the three years of this play-off competition between the respective league champions of Scotland and England in the late 'eighties. The opposition on both occasions was the same, the mighty Liverpool.

In the inaugural competition, the English champions won the cup in a penalty decider following a draw. Appropriately, the tables were turned in the same manner on the second occasion, on which Celtic went into battle on the strength of their momentous championship victory in the preceding Centenary season. The success of that historic campaign was underlined by a 4-2 triumph on penalties over the Merseysiders in Dubai in April 1989 after the match had ended at 1-1.

The magnificent golden trophy has resided at Celtic Park since that date, the competition having lapsed in the intervening years.

Height: 21"

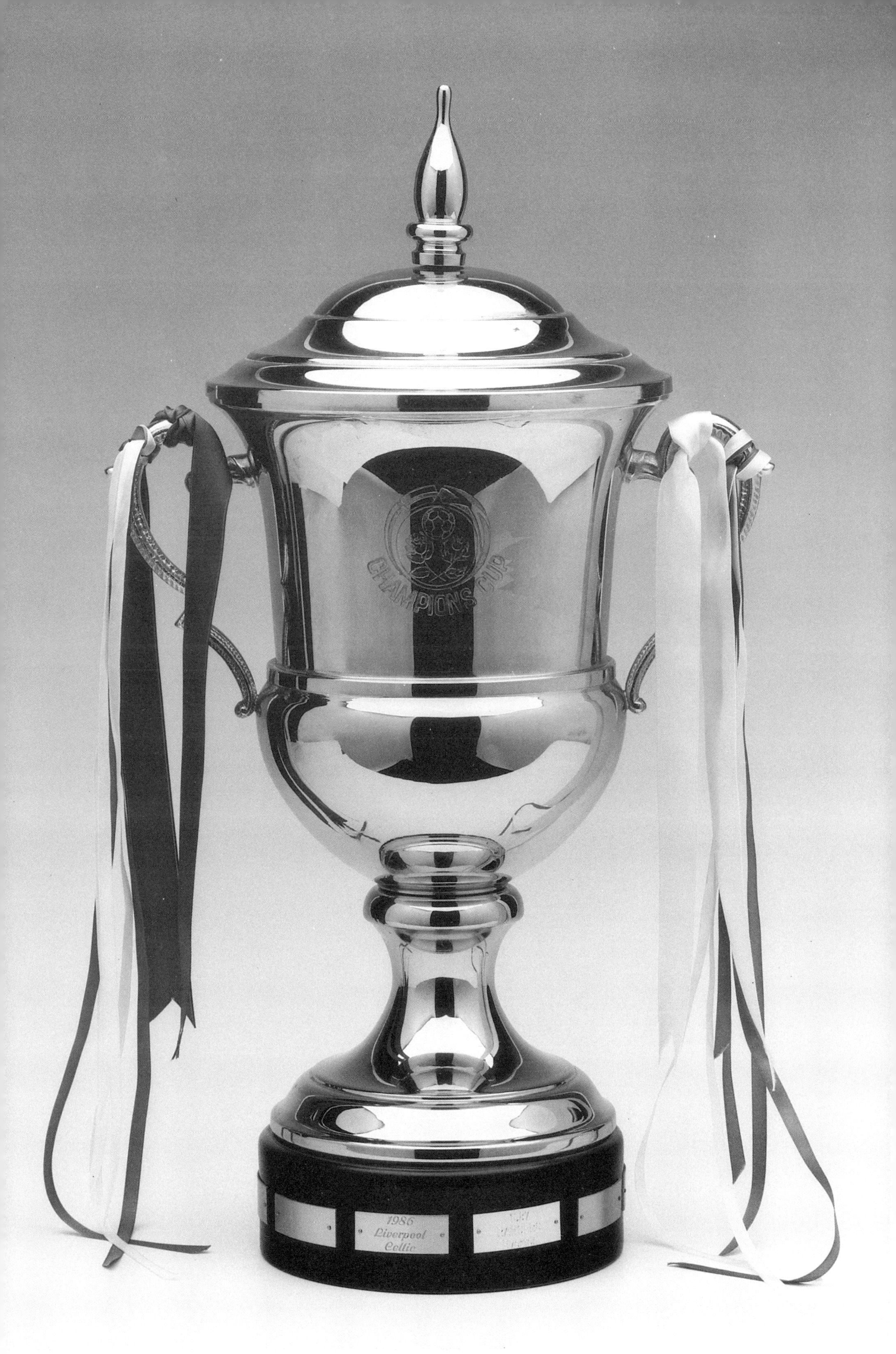
CHAMPIONS CUP
1986
Liverpool
Celtic

PATSY GALLAGHER

PATSY GALLACHER
1911-1926

The legendary Patsy Gallacher was probably the most complete footballer of his era, which is as much as any player can hope to achieve. Phenomenal dribbling, passing and shooting skills marked him out as a man ahead of his time. Allied to uncanny ball control and a tackling ability which belied his frail stature, his collective qualities made Patsy truly unique.

Probably the most enduring of his many celebrated feats is the mazy run in the 1925 Scottish Cup Final which culminated in a somersault over the goal line with the ball clutched between his feet for the equalising goal against Dundee. Celtic went on to win 2-1 over the stunned Taysiders.

Patsy's portrait is set off here by one of his many medals.

Cabinet Size: 20" x 16"

POLAR BEAR TROPHY
1975

This rather unusual and slightly gruesome memento of the Cup Winners' Cup first round confrontation with Valur of Iceland in season 1975/76 portrays the Arctic in the raw.

A solid 2-0 away win on a heavily-sanded first leg pitch put Celtic on easy street and allowed them to 'play the polar bear' with Valur at Celtic Park two weeks later. The seven Celtic goals were shared by six players, only Harry Hood managing a second.

Interestingly, Johannes 'Shuggie' Edvaldsson, Celtic's popular Icelandic internationalist of the time, directly opposed his brother in both legs. He also contrived to miss a twice-taken penalty in the first match!

September 16th: **First Leg**   Valur 0   Celtic 2
                                                                                Wilson (7)
                                                                                MacDonald (64)

Celtic: Latchford; McGrain, Lynch; McCluskey, MacDonald, Edvaldsson; Hood (Glavin), McNamara, Dalglish, Callaghan, Wilson.

October 1st: **Second Leg**   Celtic 7   Valur 0
                                                                      Edvaldsson (6)
                                                                      Dalglish (12)
                                                                      P. McCluskey, pen. (30)
                                                                      Hood (37, 82)
                                                                      Deans (42)
                                                                      Callaghan (50)

Celtic: Latchford; McGrain, Lynch; P. McCluskey, MacDonald, Edvaldsson; Wilson (G. McCluskey), Dalglish, Deans, Callaghan (Casey), Hood.

Height: 10"

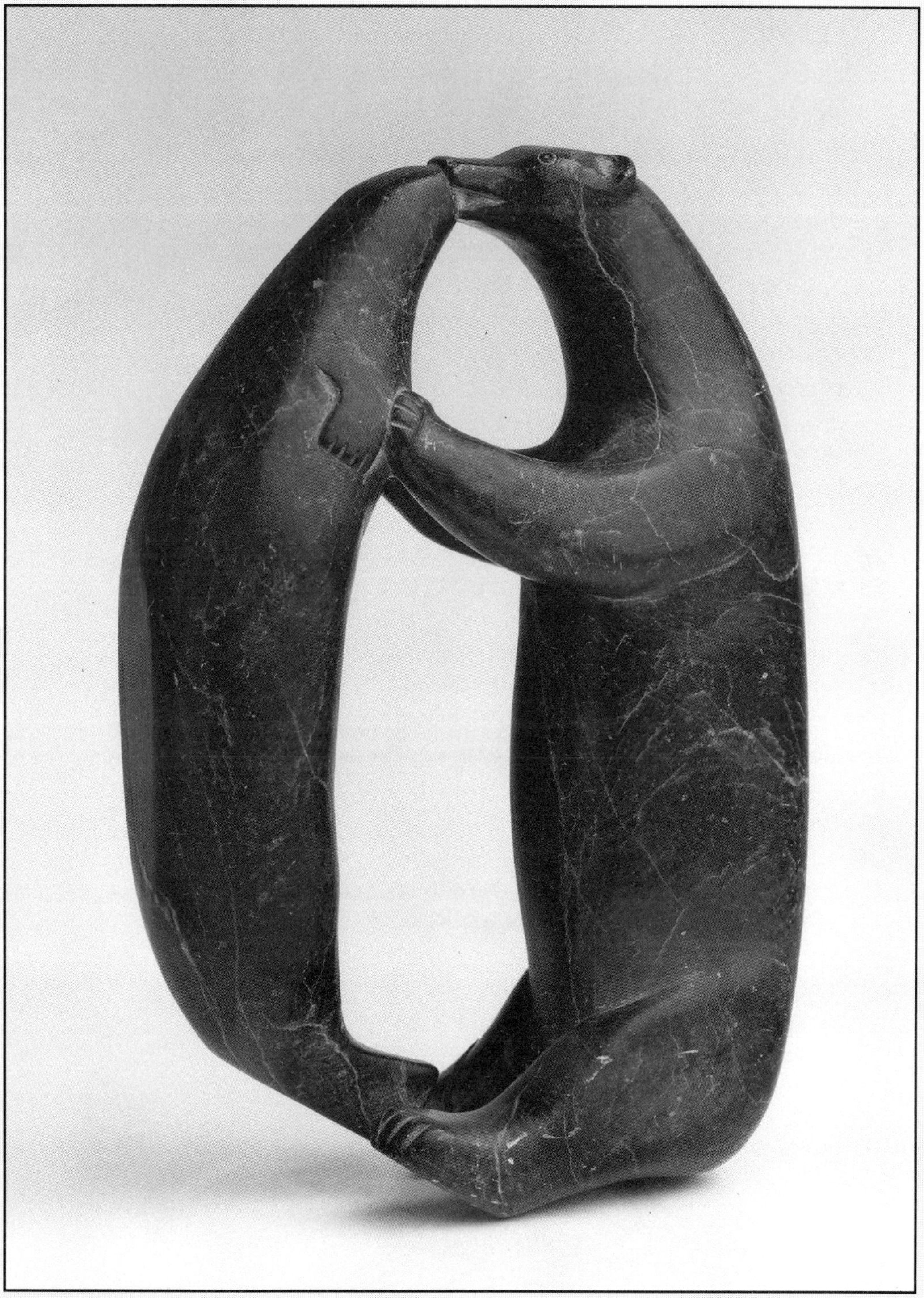

THE ST MUNGO CUP
1951

One of the most distinctive of the many trophies housed at Celtic Park, the St Mungo Cup was tinged with controversy. Coming in the wake of a lengthy barren spell, mercifully ended by the capture of the Scottish Cup of season 1950/51 and hard upon the club's return from a second epic North American tour, the competition formed part of the 'Festival of Britain' celebrations.

Organised jointly by Glasgow Corporation and the Scottish Football Association, the event involved all sixteen clubs of the then First Division. When the dust settled, Celtic and Aberdeen had duly qualified to face each other in the final on August 1st.

Celtic started badly and fell two goals behind. However, a second-half revival produced goals from Walsh, Fallon and Tully to turn what had looked like a lost cause into yet another 'one-off' triumph.

Behind the celebrations, though, was the whiff of parsimony. The handles of the curiously-constructed trophy had been fashioned in the shape of a salmon, one of the emblems of Glasgow. When one of these handles came away in a Celtic hand, suspicions were aroused as to the trophy's pedigree.

*Investigations showed that the St Mungo Cup was, at best, second-hand! Dating back to 1894, its history was somewhat hazy, though it **was** known to have been the object of a match between Provan Gasworks and Glasgow Police. For the record, the Gasworks were victorious!*

Apparently, some luminary had conceived a plan to refurbish and recycle the relic as a cut-price 'St Mungo Cup'. Despite Celtic's understandable protestations, no replacement was made and so it is that the hybrid trophy retains a prominent place in the main trophy cabinet at Celtic Park.

The St Mungo Cup winners were: Hunter; Haughney, Rollo; Evans, Mallan, Baillie; Collins, Walsh, Fallon, Peacock, Tully.

Height: 25"

FESTIVAL OF BRITAIN
1951
THE ST MUNGO CUP
PRESENTED BY
THE LORD PROVOST
AND
CORPORATION
OF GLASGOW

R.M.S. CELTIC
White Star Line
1901-1928

This painting was unearthed amongst a long-forgotten cache during renovations a few years ago. Stadium Director Tom Grant resisted the temptation to dispose of an undistinguishable piece of apparent junk and you can imagine his delight when restoration work revealed its identity.

The 'Celtic' ploughed the transatlantic route between Liverpool and New York, sometimes docking at Cork, on the southern coast of Ireland. The liner foundered on the rocks at Roche's Point off Cobh Island, the traditional departure point for Irish emigrants to the 'New World', while attempting to berth during a storm in December 1928.

In the course of the subsequent salvage operation, many of the fittings mysteriously found their way into the homes and premises of the little village of Ringaskiddy, near Cork, including the ship's bell, which ended up in the oratory of the local church. Celtic F.C. directors tried unsuccessfully to buy the bell during a tour visit for a match against Cobh Ramblers.

It was not to be but at least the glorious painting of the vessel which proudly bore the name 'Celtic' is there for all to see and enjoy.

Dimensions: 26" x 40"

BOAVISTA CARAVEL
1975

A fine away second round performance in Portugal, which featured a remarkable goalkeeping display by Peter Latchford (including a magnificent penalty stop five minutes from time), set Celtic up for the European Cup Winners' Cup quarter-finals of season 1975/76.

The Celtic Park return leg was wrapped up five minutes from time by the third goal, scored by 'Dixie' Deans from a Dalglish through ball. Celtic won 3-1 on aggregate.

October 22nd: **First Leg**   Boavista 0   Celtic 0

Celtic: Latchford; McGrain, Lynch; P. McCluskey, MacDonald, Edvaldsson; Callaghan, McNamara, Wilson, Hood, Lennox.

November 5th: **Second Leg**   Celtic 3   Boavista 1
Dalglish (35 secs)
Edvaldsson (20)
Deans (85)

Celtic: Latchford; McGrain, Lynch; P. McCluskey, MacDonald, Edvaldsson; G. McCluskey, Dalglish, Deans, McNamara, Callaghan (Lennox).

Height: 10"

1901
QUEEN'S PARK, RANGERS, CELTIC, 3RD LANARK,
HEART OF MIDLOTHIAN, HIBERNIAN, ST MIRREN, MORTON,
AND WON BY
RANGERS F.C.

GLASGOW EXHIBITION CUP
1901/02

The story of how Celtic came into possession of this extravagant silver confection is the perfect example of cashing in on a second bite at the cherry.

As the object of strenuous competition amongst eight of Scotland's leading clubs in the football tournament which marked the Glasgow International Exhibition of 1901, the trophy was originally won by already intense rivals, Rangers, in a bruising, controversial final against (who else?) Celtic. Proving that nothing really changes that much, the aftermath was a familiar battery of counter allegations.

The following year was blighted by the dreadful disaster at Ibrox when dozens were killed and hundreds injured in a terracing collapse during the April Scotland v England international.

As part of a massive effort throughout Scottish and English football to compensate victims and rescue both Rangers and the S.F.A. from perilous financial straits, a competition was arranged amongst the reigning champions of Scotland and England (Rangers and Sunderland) and the respective runners-up (Celtic and Everton). Press hype built the tournament into a British Championship and Rangers decided to raise the stakes by putting up their Exhibition Cup as a permanent prize for the winners.

Almost inevitably, Celtic dispatched Sunderland, Rangers overcame Everton and the pair came face to face again in what William Maley recalled (in his book, 'The Story of the Celtic') as an epic 'double-header' on June 17th and 19th, 1902. Celtic eventually clinched the tournament and the cup with a third goal in the dying moments of extra time following a 2-2 draw.

An interesting footnote is that another Celtic/Rangers clash was arranged a couple of months later, again in aid of the Disaster Fund and sponsored by Bovril in the form of medals. The outcome, at Hampden on August 20th, was more conclusive, Celtic winning 7-2, with Jimmy Quinn banging in a hat-trick!

Height: 23½"

CITY OF GLASGOW PLAQUE
1967

Presented by the then Lord Provost, John Johnston J.P., on behalf of the City of Glasgow to mark the wonder year of 1966/67. The plaque carries the 'Let Glasgow Flourish' coat of arms and bears the outline map of Europe, fittingly embossed with the Celtic club crest, symbolic of their dominance at that time.

The shield records the team's triumphs and bears the names of the Celtic personnel involved, from playing and backroom staff through to management and directors.

That magical season was the most successful in the club's illustrious history, as Celtic won every competition entered. This included the domestic 'treble' and of course, the European Champions' Cup itself, won by a British (and non-latin) club for the first time, making Celtic the envy of every major club in the country.

Diameter: 19$\frac{1}{2}$"

EUROPEAN CUP WINNERS
1967
CELTIC FOOTBALL CLUB
1888
SCOTTISH LEAGUE
SCOTTISH CUP
SCOTTISH LEAGUE CUP
GLASGOW CUP
The City of Glasgow

VALENCIA TROPHY
1962

The first round, first leg of the Fairs Cities Cup of season 1962/63 saw Celtic beaten 4-2 by Valencia C.F. in Spain. Some hope remained, however, for the home return leg thanks to a Bobby Carroll double in a creditable Celtic display.

A Celtic Park crowd of 45,000 was bitterly disappointed, though, by a lacklustre 2-2 draw, which was, in truth, no more than was deserved. John Clark's early penalty miss set the tone for a sad night and only a late Pat Crerand strike saved an embarrassing home defeat. However, the Spaniards went home 6-4 aggregate winners.

They left only this elegant memento.

September 26th: **First Leg**   Valencia 4   Celtic 2
Carroll 2

Celtic: Fallon; McKay, Kennedy; Crerand, McNeill, O'Neill; Chalmers, Jackson, Carroll, Gallagher, Byrne.

October 24th: **Second Leg**   Celtic 2   Valencia 2
Verdu, o.g. (48)
Crerand (85)

Celtic: Haffey; McKay, O'Neill; Crerand, McNamee, Clark; Chalmers, Craig, Divers, Gallagher, Byrne.

Height: 12"

V. COPA FERIAS
CELTIC F.C.-VALENCIA C.F.
VALENCIA. SEPTIEMBRE 1962

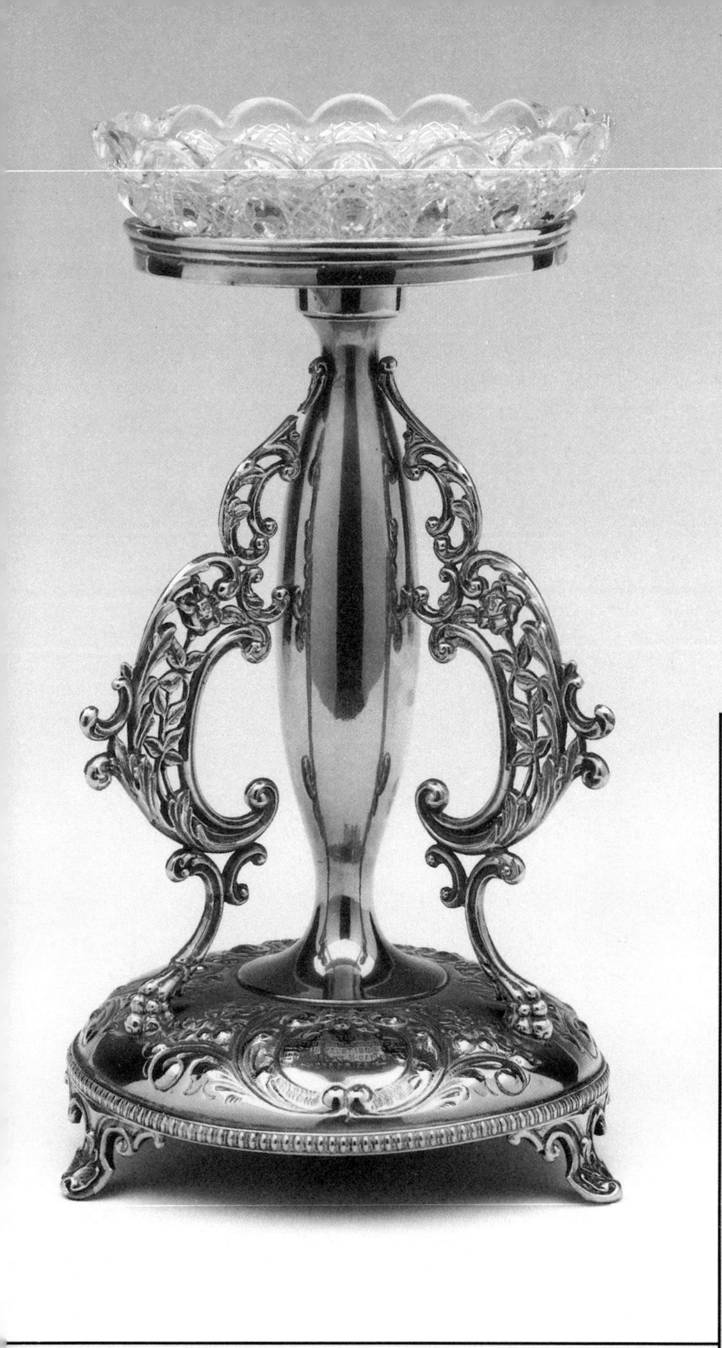

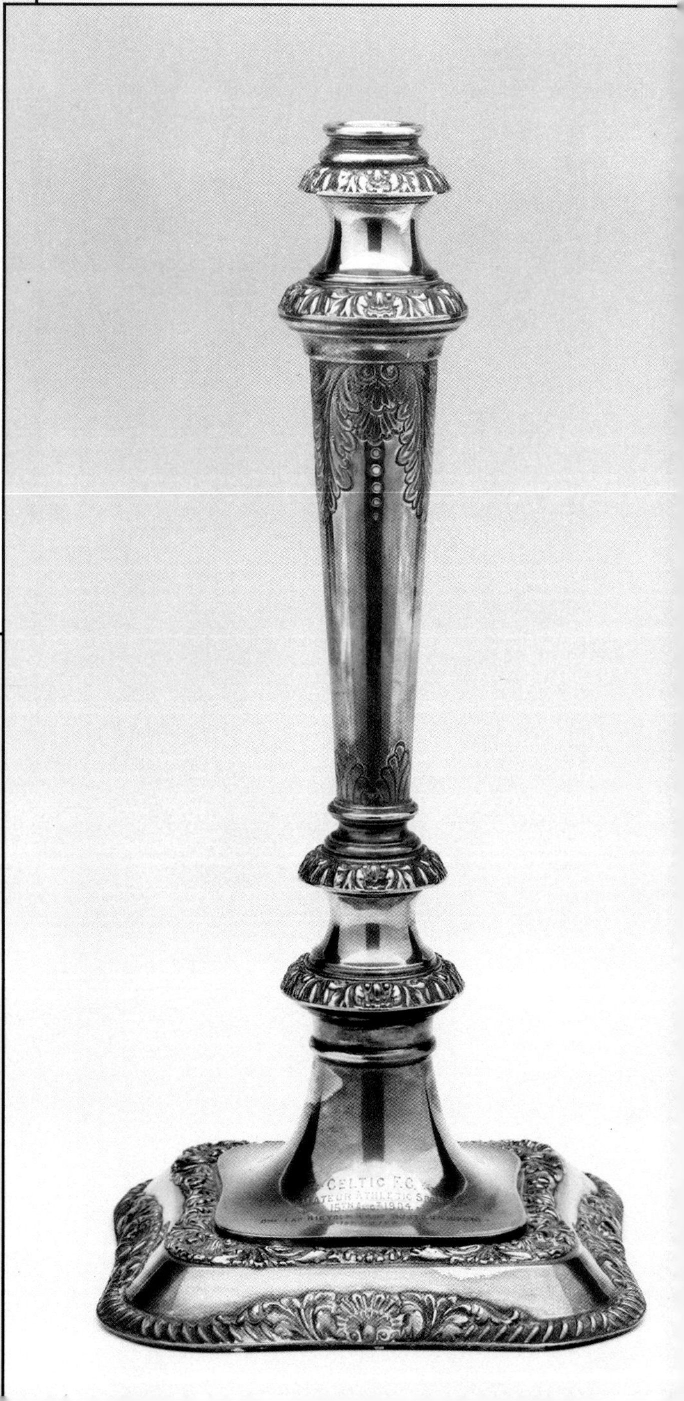
CELTIC F.C.

ATHLETICS TROPHY/CYCLING TROPHY
1904

The rather quaint old trophies depicted opposite (Athletics, above) recall those long-forgotten days around the turn of the century when athletics and cycling enjoyed considerably more mass appeal in the West of Scotland than they now command outwith the glamorous televised meetings. In keeping with the club's early pioneering instincts, Celtic were at the forefront in giving the public what it wanted and from 1890 onwards, the Celtic Sports became an increasing highlight of the sporting calendar.

At their height, these meetings attracted athletes and cyclists from not only all over Scotland but indeed from all over the world. To win a Celtic Handicap was a fervent athletic ambition.

Cycling first took place in a limited way on the primitive dirt track of the old ground at the corner of Janefield Street and Dalmarnock Street. Its popularity led to the special provision of a red cinder track when the new Celtic Park was being laid down. This was subsequently upgraded to a special cement track, an innovation in Scotland at the time.

These efforts were rewarded by the first and only staging in Scotland of the World Cycling Championships at Celtic Park in 1898.

Heights: Athletics 12"/Cycling 14 1/2"

CENTENARY GAME

CELTIC V CRUZEIRO
7th August, 1988.
Sponsored By
STRATHVALE HOMES

CENTENARY CUP
1988

Amongst the various events held to commemorate the club's Centenary year was a special match against the most glamorous opposition, the colourful Brazilians of Cruzeiro Belo Horizonte. The game took place on August 7th 1988, with Celtic, fittingly, the reigning Scottish Premier League Champions and Scottish Cup holders.

As you would expect, the 'centurions' of Parkhead held their heads high and ensured a rightful home at Celtic Park for the Centenary Cup, treating the fans to a thrilling 4-2 victory, featuring an Andy Walker hat-trick and a typical Frank McAvennie counter.

The Celtic team on a famous occasion was: Andrews, Morris, Rogan, Aitken, McCarthy, Grant, Miller, McStay, McAvennie, Walker, Burns.

Height: 13½"

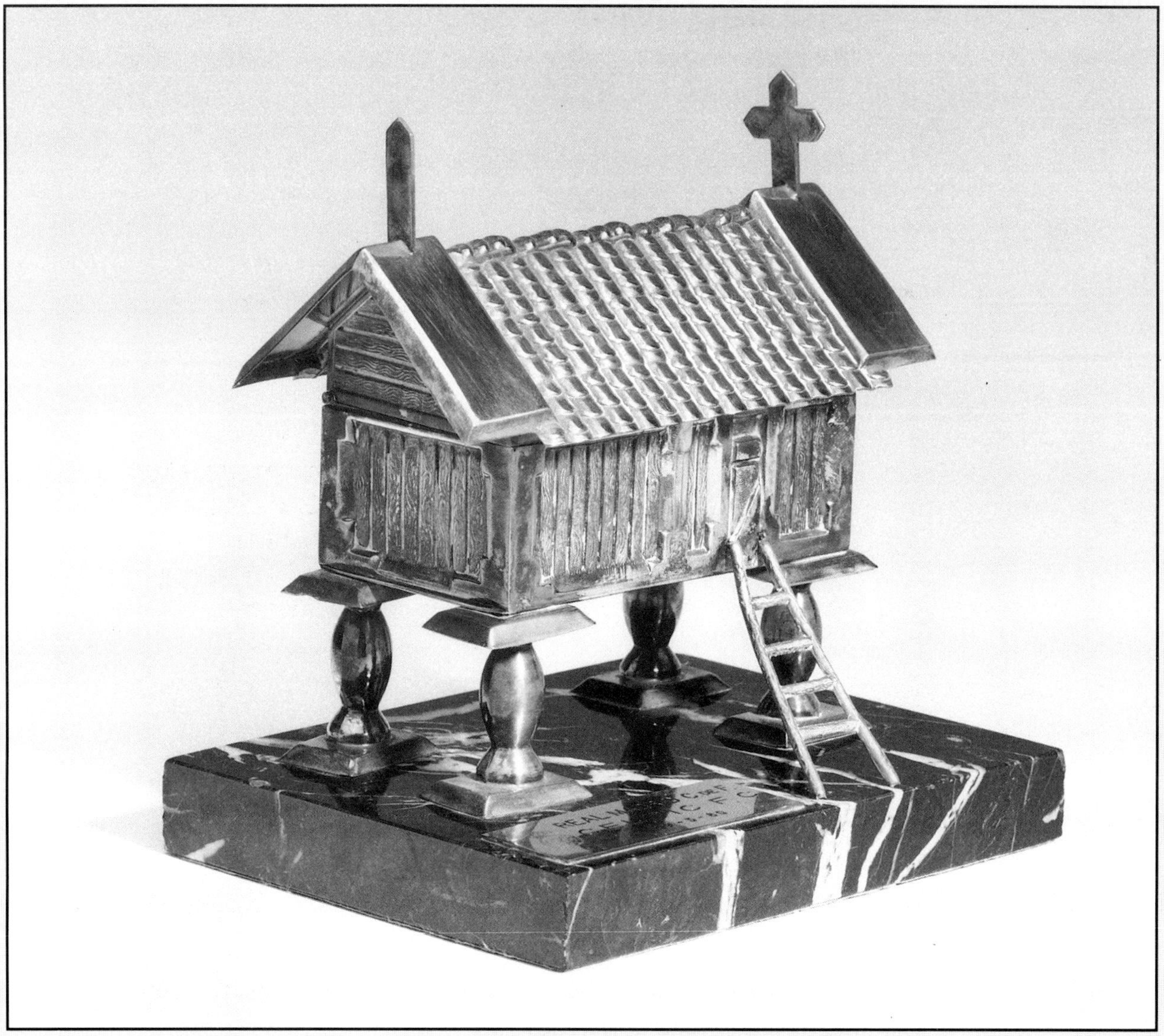

REAL MADRID SILVER CABIN
1980

The mighty Real Madrid presented this unusual and beautifully-crafted memento of a pulsating European Cup quarter-final in season 1979/80.

Celtic powered their way to a 2-0 first leg lead through a flawless second half performance which brought goals, first from George McCluskey and then John Doyle. The second was a high-leaping header, quite untypical of the fiery little winger.

An early golden chance to set up a famous victory was spurned in the second leg before Real went on to clinch the tie, producing super skills allied to a 'robust' approach which was encouraged by some indulgent refereeing, to run out 3-2 aggregate winners. Not before Celtic had given them a few more frights, however, most notably when a solid penalty claim for handling was denied and Pirri almost put a pass-back through his own goal.

March 5th: **First Leg**   Celtic 2   Real Madrid 0
                                         McCluskey (52)
                                         Doyle (74)

Celtic: Latchford; Sneddon, McGrain; Aitken, McAdam, MacDonald; MacLeod, Provan, Lennox, McCluskey, Doyle.

March 19th: **Second Leg**   Real Madrid 3   Celtic 0

Celtic: Latchford; Sneddon, McAdam, MacDonald, McGrain; Provan, Aitken, Doyle; MacLeod, McCluskey (Burns), Lennox.

Height: 5½"

SCOTTISH LEAGUE PLAQUE
1972

Awarded by the Scottish Football League, this fine ornamental piece of onyx is tangible recognition of Celtic's seven successive League Championships from 1965/66 - 1971/72. The feat overtook the club's own historic record run of six titles in a row by the epic sides of 1904/05 - 1909/10.

In reality, however, the award was somewhat premature as the 'sixties/ 'seventies run was extended for a further two seasons into a world record equalling 'nine-in-a-row', which phenomenal achievement was never properly acknowledged by a formal presentation.

Nevertheless, the gracious award is rightly treasured as a symbol of Celtic's proud tradition of setting the standards to which others must aspire.

Height: 13"

TEAM POOL PLATE
Season 1913/14

Over the years, the club has been contacted by countless fans offering a copy of this fine plate for display, clearly thinking that they were in possession of a scarce and valuable object. So much so, one must conclude that some clever entrepreneur of the time did a good job of producing and distributing these souvenirs.

It is, nevertheless, an attractive and fascinating relic of bygone days.

Prominent amongst the group are manager Maley and a youngish Patsy Gallacher (second from left, front row).

Diameter: 8"

Presented by
The Glasgow Charity Cup Committee
to Commemorate
Victory in Europe
9th May 1945
Match at Hampden Park
Celtic v Queen's Park

VICTORY IN EUROPE CUP
1945

Celtic's only wartime honours were the Glasgow Cup of 1940/41 and the Charity Cup of 1942/43. This comparative famine may in part be explained by the club's steadfast refusal to follow the fashion of strengthening their ranks with displaced guest-stars stationed locally under the prevailing emergency conditions.

However, when the Glasgow Charity Cup committee put up this handsome trophy to raise money for war charities, the 'Bhoys' rose to the occasion, winning the trophy outright at Hampden against Queen's Park on May 9th 1945. The opposition should have been Rangers but the Govan club declined the invitation on account of having another cup final the following week.

The match actually ended at 1-1 but these were the days in which the respective number of corner kicks won were sometimes used to decide drawn games. Celtic had gained a single corner advantage and this was enough to ensure another 'one-off' award for the Parkhead trophy collection.

The victorious Celtic team was: Miller; Hogg, P. McDonald; Lynch, Mallan, McPhail; Paton, M. MacDonald, Gallacher, Evans, McLaughlin.

Bobby Hogg and Malcolm MacDonald had also played in the Empire Exhibition team of 1938.

Height: 14½"

FERENCVAROS VASE
1914/1988

Celtic had from the outset brought a pioneering spirit to football. By the turn of the century they were ready to carry the gospel further afield, undertaking a series of trips across Europe, virgin territory for a Scottish club.

On one such expedition to Hungary in 1914, the local Budapest club, Ferencvarosi Torna, presented a splendid trophy for charity competition between Celtic (who had not been consulted in advance) and English touring side Burnley.

All ill-tempered match ended in a draw and could not be replayed as Celtic were returning to Scotland next day. Amidst the resultant mayhem, the teams refused to play extra time and the trophy was withheld. A compromise was reached to play the game off in Britain, with Burnley gaining home advantage on the toss of a coin.

Celtic duly travelled to Burnley, overturned the English side 2-0 and claimed their prize. Unfortunately, despite several representations and full compliance with the agreement to forward part of the gate money to the Hungarian charity fund, the trophy never materialised. Subsequent investigations revealed that it had been disposed of in a fund-raising venture during World War I.

The happy sequel to this story is that the latter-day officials of Ferencvaros, being aware of Celtic's Centenary and realising that the historic victory had never been properly marked, decided to set matters straight. A party flew over for Celtic's Centenary Championship-clinching match against Dundee at Celtic Park in April 1988 to present this truly magnificent replacement.

Height: 19½"

PRESENTED BY
FERENCVÁROS BUDAPEST
TO
CELTIC FOOTBALL CLUB
IN THEIR CENTENARY YEAR
TO MARK THEIR FIRST
"EUROPEAN CUP" VICTORY
IN 1914
/RESULTS FOR THE CUP WERE
CELTIC - BURNLEY,
DRAW IN BUDAPEST
BURNLEY- CELTIC ,0-2 IN BURNLEY/

7 TH MAY, 1988

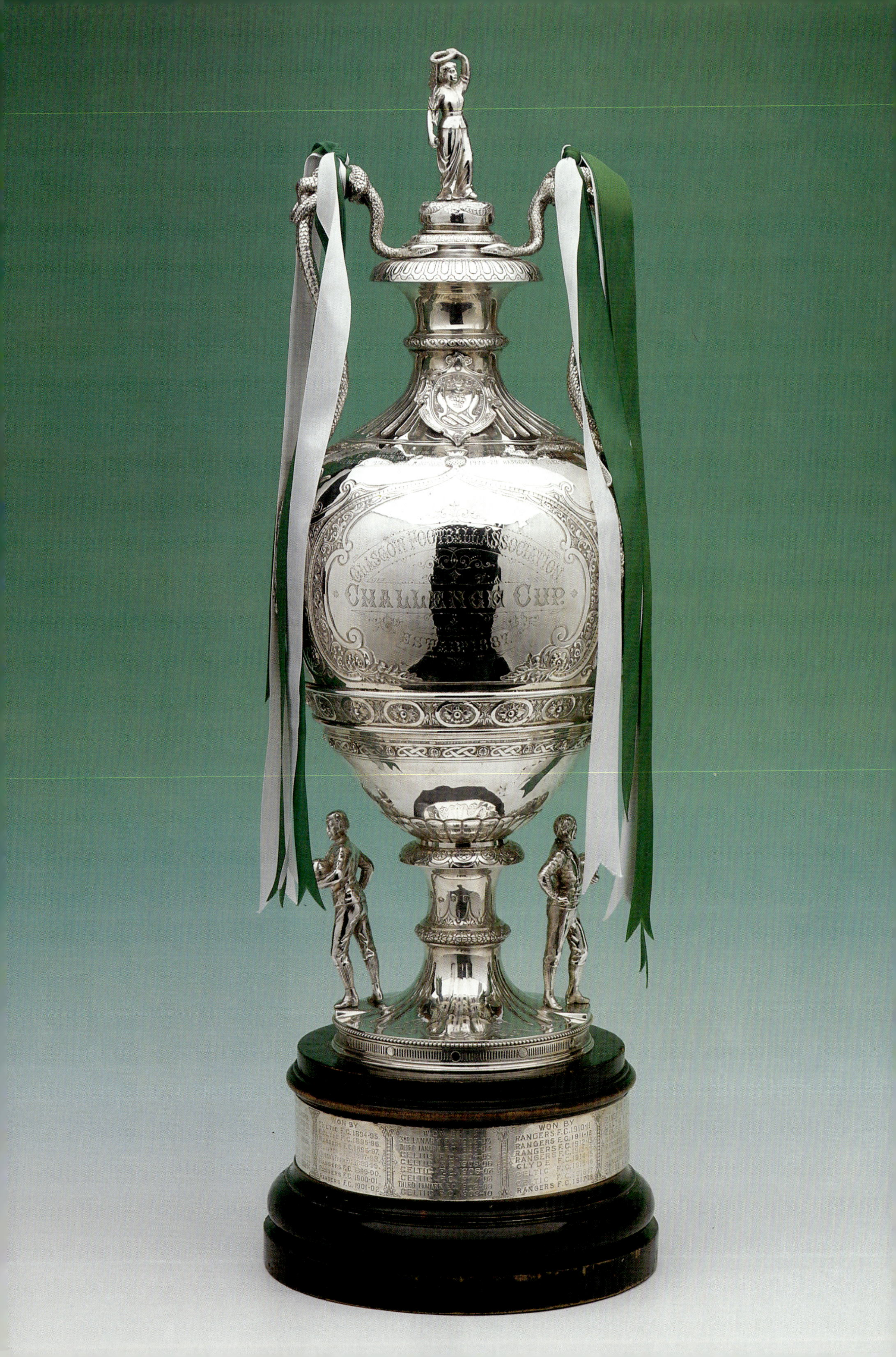
GLASGOW FOOTBALL ASSOCIATION
CHALLENGE CUP

THE GLASGOW CUP

This spectacular trophy, which once ranked, together with the Glasgow Charity Cup (present whereabouts unknown), amongst Scotland's premier senior football competitions, was won by Celtic twenty-nine times in its heyday. In those days, Glasgow Cup matches, featuring such now-sadly-defunct outfits as Third Lanark as well as Celtic, Rangers and the other senior Glasgow clubs, attracted crowds to rival any event in the football calendar. It was a tournament of genuine prestige, as its imposing appearance proudly proclaims.

Sadly, with the passage of time, the Glasgow Cup drifted into something of a non-event, as the advent of European football, with the glamorous occasions generated, drew the focus away from minor domestic competition. A once-proud contest had become something of a joke, paid scant attention by clubs and public alike.

Only in recent years has the historic old 'pot' had some of its former pride, if not prestige, restored. It is now contested by the young lions of the Glasgow clubs' under-18 sides and keenly contested at that, attracting large, enthusiastic crowds looking for an early glimpse of the stars of the future. In the first two years of this competition, the trophy was won and retained by the young Celts.

Surely the Glasgow Cup could find no more noble destiny than to inspire and elevate ambitious young footballers at the threshold of their careers!

Height: 31½"

FRANCE-FOOTBALL ADIDAS
CHALLENGE EUROPÉEN DE FOOTBALL 1970
CELTIC - GLASGOW

STATUETTE OF SAMOTHRACE
1970

In this exquisite figurine, Celtic can boast a genuine objet d'art. The statuette is a replica of the very famous sculpture housed in the renowned L'Ouvre Museum in Paris.

Presented by the prestigious French sports newspaper 'France Football', it commemorates Celtic's selection as 'European Team of the Year' for general performance in season 1969/70. That term, the club won the League Championship by a massive twelve point margin, lifted the League Cup for a remarkable fifth successive year and was runner-up in both the Scottish and European Cups.

To win this competition, which is still in operation, is quite an accolade, as it is based on clubs' combined records in all domestic and European games throughout each season. Only the cream can compete — only the ***great*** *win!*

Height: 12"

PRESENTED TO THE
CELTIC FOOTBALL CLUB
- BY THE -
UNITED STATES FOOTBALL ASSOCIATION Inc.
ON THE OCCASION OF
THEIR UNITED STATES TOUR
- 1931 -

U.S. TOURS

Celtic Football Club has a long-standing tradition of crossing the Atlantic for summer tours. Indeed, one such tour, in the summer of 1966, is generally considered the springboard to the phenomenal achievements of the ensuing season.

Indian Chief
1931

Another superb statuette, presented to Celtic by the United States Football Association to mark the 1931 summer tour by the then Scottish Cup holders. The tour matches were centred on Pennsylvania, New York and Baltimore.

*Celtic suffered an unlikely 1-0 defeat at the hands of Fall River, a result inspired by a magnificent display in goal by one Joe Kennaway. It was no mere coincidence that **he** was the man chosen to replace the legendary John Thomson following the tragic premature death of the goalkeeping genius.*

Tour Record:	Played	Won	Lost	Drawn	For	Against
	13	9	3	1	48	18

Height: 13³⁄₄"

GLASGOW CELTIC F. C.
1951
UNITED STATES TOUR
Celtic Ties Fulham, 1-All, In Brilliant Soccer Show
BY ED WARING
BLACK
LOWE
TAYLOR
McPHAIL
WELCOME GLASGOW CELTIC
AMERICAN LEAGUE SOCCER NEWS
MAY 20, 1951
No Charge
UNITED STATES WELCOMES GLASGOW CELTIC WINNER OF SCOTTISH CUP HEADS GREAT INTERNATIONAL SCHEDULE
GLASGOW CELTIC Vs. FULHAM NEXT SUNDAY
1951 WINNERS OF SCOTTISH CUP
GLASGOW CELTIC
OFFICIAL
SCOT'S AMERICAN A. C.
Tickets for Glasgow Celtic—Fulham Game on Sale After Today's Game at Ticket Booths in Triboro Stadium Lobby.

U.S. TOURS

Tour Archive
1951

Twenty years after the first transatlantic trip, Celtic again headed west as Scottish Cup holders, co-incidentally having defeated the same opponents, Motherwell, at Hampden to bring down the curtain on a nightmare thirteen year period without a major national trophy.

This book contains fascinating press cuttings which provide an intriguing insight into the events of another socially rumbustious tour. On-field trouble flared and fists flew during the match in New York with Eintracht of Germany, who became incensed at three penalty awards against them. Otherwise the tour was comparatively routine, except for the novelty of television promotional appearances and a meeting with a genuine Red Indian chief who was said to be 120 years old.

Tour Record:	Played	Won	Lost	Drawn	For	Against
	9	7	1	1	27	9

THE EMPIRE EXHIBITION TROPHY
1938

Falling into the same 'one-off' category as the Coronation Cup, the distinctive Empire Exhibition Trophy was the subject of an earlier Scotland/England joust to mark the great Empire Exhibition of 1938, happily coinciding with Celtic's Golden Jubilee.

Amidst the royal pomp and ceremony which saw King George VI at Ibrox Park for the opening ceremony on May 3rd, a major football competition was organised. Celtic, Rangers, Hearts and Aberdeen were ranged against formidable English opposition in Sunderland, Chelsea, Brentford and Everton.

The Exhibition itself was a major public attraction, drawing huge crowds to Bellahouston Park and its surrounds. This public response was equally reflected in the football matches, all of which were played at Ibrox.

Celtic's opening tie, a goalless draw with Sunderland, was attended by a crowd of 54,000. The match was replayed the following evening, with Celtic progressing to face Hearts in the next round thanks to goals from Divers (2) and Crum.

Another Crum goal, the only score of the game, took Celtic through against Hearts to meet the might of Everton (who had earlier dumped both Aberdeen and Rangers) in the final on June 10th. Consider the magnitude of Celtic's task — Everton had at their disposal no fewer than ten internationalists, drawn from all four home countries!

A splendid final was witnessed by a worthy crowd of 82,000 spectators. The Celtic goal, stoutly defended by Joe Kennaway, was under constant threat from the legendary Tommy Lawton. The great centre-forward's efforts came to nothing, however, as did Celtic's and the regulation ninety minutes yielded no score. Seven minutes into extra time, however, Johnny Crum fired home his third goal of the competition, which proved conclusive and secured another majestic and permanent trophy.

Celtic legend, Jimmy Delaney, always maintained that the side which conquered Everton that day was the best in which he ever played.

The great side was: Kennaway; Hogg, Morrison; Geatons, Lyon, Paterson; Delaney, MacDonald, Crum, Divers, Murphy.

Height: 23"

FOOTBALL·COMPETITION·TROPHY
PRESENTED BY
THE EMPIRE EXHIBITION (SCOTLAND), 1938.
TO BE THE ABSOLUTE PROPERTY OF THE WINNER
CELTIC FOOTBALL CLUB

FEYENOORD CLOCK
1970

If Celtic's most glorious moment came in a European Cup Final, so too did one of their blackest, just three years later.

Perhaps expectations had been unrealistically high following the epic semi-final triumph over Don Revie's powerful Leeds United. Dubbed 'the final before the final', that tie had seen Celtic at their majestic best, overcoming the strongly-fancied English champions home and away.

Whatever the reason, in the final itself Feyenoord were much the more competent side on the day, proving themselves a far better team than anyone had expected.

May 6th: **Final**   Celtic 1   Feyenoord 2
Gemmell (30)

Celtic: Williams; Hay, Gemmell; Murdoch, McNeill, Brogan; Johnstone, Lennox, Wallace, Auld (Connelly), Hughes.

Height: 22½"

JOHN GLASS
Founder Member and First President

No less an authority than the great William Maley, in 'The Story of The Celtic', accredits John Glass with being the man to whom The Celtic Football Club owes its very existence. According to Maley, who was a first-hand witness to those early events, if Brother Walfrid was the inspiration behind the club's formation, then Glass was the powerhouse whose tireless devotion to the cause helped ensure that the dream became reality.

This is not, of course, to diminish the role of any of the other founding fathers, as remarkable and doggedly determined a group of idealists as ever came together in sporting enterprise. Rather it is to apportion to Glass an appropriate measure of credit and to start to explain the pre-eminent position of his portrait at the head of the Celtic Park central staircase.

Glass, a powerful man of Donegal stock and a well-contacted joiner in the building trade, was one of the group of three (the others being Brother Walfrid himself and Pat 'Tailor' Welsh, another prospering immigrant Irish businessman) who were responsible for bringing William Maley into the Celtic camp. In truth, it was only an impulse of Brother Walfrid's, impressed by the youngster's attitude when he, Glass and Welsh called at the Maley home to secure the playing services of brother Tom, who was not there at the time. This was long before Celtic ever put a team in the field.

The rest, of course, is Celtic history, though the playing exploits of the Maley brothers were insignificant by comparison with the legendary management record of William.

John Glass died in 1906, by which time he had seen Brother Walfrid's vision bear fruit in a dominant Celtic Football Club, though it had soon outgrown its original parochial charity format into the embryo of the organisation we know today.

Dimensions: 48" x 35 3/4"

THE EUROPEAN CHAMPIONS' CUP
'The Campaign'
1966-1967

First Round:	**1st Leg**	Celtic 2	F. C. Zurich 0
	2nd Leg	F.C. Zurich 0	Celtic 3
Second Round:	**1st Leg**	C. F. Nantes 1	Celtic 3
	2nd Leg	Celtic 3	C. F. Nantes 1
Quarter Final:	**1st Leg**	Vojvodina Novi Sad 1	Celtic 0
	2nd Leg	Celtic 2	Vojvodina Novi Sad 0
Semi Final:	**1st Leg**	Celtic 3	Dukla Prague 1
	2nd Leg	Dukla Prague 0	Celtic 0

Final: **Estadio Nacional, Lisbon**
May 25th 1967. Attendance 55,000

Celtic 2   Internazionale Milan 1

ISRAELI COPPER VASE
1970

On Wednesday, May 26th 1970, Celtic took part in an exhibition match in Tel Aviv against a Hapoel Select side which was a virtual Israeli international eleven. The game was played in the National Stadium before a crowd of 33,000 spectators. Celtic won the closely-contested match 1-0 thanks to a first-half Harry Hood strike.

A grateful Israeli Football Association commemorated Celtic's visit with this unusual ornament.

The Celtic team for the occasion was: Williams; Hay, McGrain; Callaghan, McNeill, Connelly; Johnstone, Hood, Macari, Dalglish, Lennox.

Height: 14½"

FEYENOORD JUG
1981

Celtic's old European adversaries of bitter recollection hosted a highly-prestigious pre-season tournament in the run-up to the 1981/82 campaign. Our Dutch hosts presented this distinctive jug as a memento of the occasion.

A small measure of retribution was exacted for former discomfiture through a semi-final victory over Feyenoord as Celtic went on to win the tournament with a fine 2-1 triumph over Dukla Prague of Czechoslovakia.

Happier recollections surrounded that final match, of course, Dukla having been the semi-final opposition in the glorious European Cup campaign of 1966/67 (see pages 28 and 84).

Height: 15¼"

John Thomson Memorial Cabinet.

PRESENTED
TO
THE CELTIC FOOTBALL CLUB
In commemoration of their having won
THE
CHAMPIONSHIP COMPETITION

THE LEAGUE SHIELD
1904/05-1909/10

The Centenary Championship of season 1987/88 was Celtic's thirty-fifth title. That proud record is characterised by a series of phenomenal winning streaks, interspersed with comparatively lean periods.

Having quickly established itself as a major national football power, the club proceeded to snatch four of the first eight championships from the League's inception in 1890/91. It was also runner-up twice over that period and three times in all out of the first ten years, during which the lowest finish was fourth. Not a bad start!

You could be forgiven for thinking that things could only get worse **but in fact they were soon to get even better.**

After a bit of a stutter around the turn of the century, managing only two seconds, a third and a fifth place, Celtic went on the rampage again, claiming a remarkable ten out of the next thirteen championships from 1904/05 onwards. Throw in another two second places for good measure over that period and you can see the dominance which was Celtic's at the time.

Part of the above sequence was a run of six successive titles between 1904/05 and 1909/10, a feat immortalised by the Scottish Football League through the presentation of the magnificent silver-encrusted shield pictured here. The names of the players from each successful season are inscribed in the circles surrounding the central Lion Rampant.

This impressive throwback to a more gracious age has, in recent years, been given pride of place on the new Board Room wall. The deeds which it commemorates and the dominance it represents were destined never to be equalled until the rise of that other great Celtic side of the 'sixties and 'seventies.

Dimensions: 26$^{3}/_{4}$" x 20$^{3}/_{4}$"

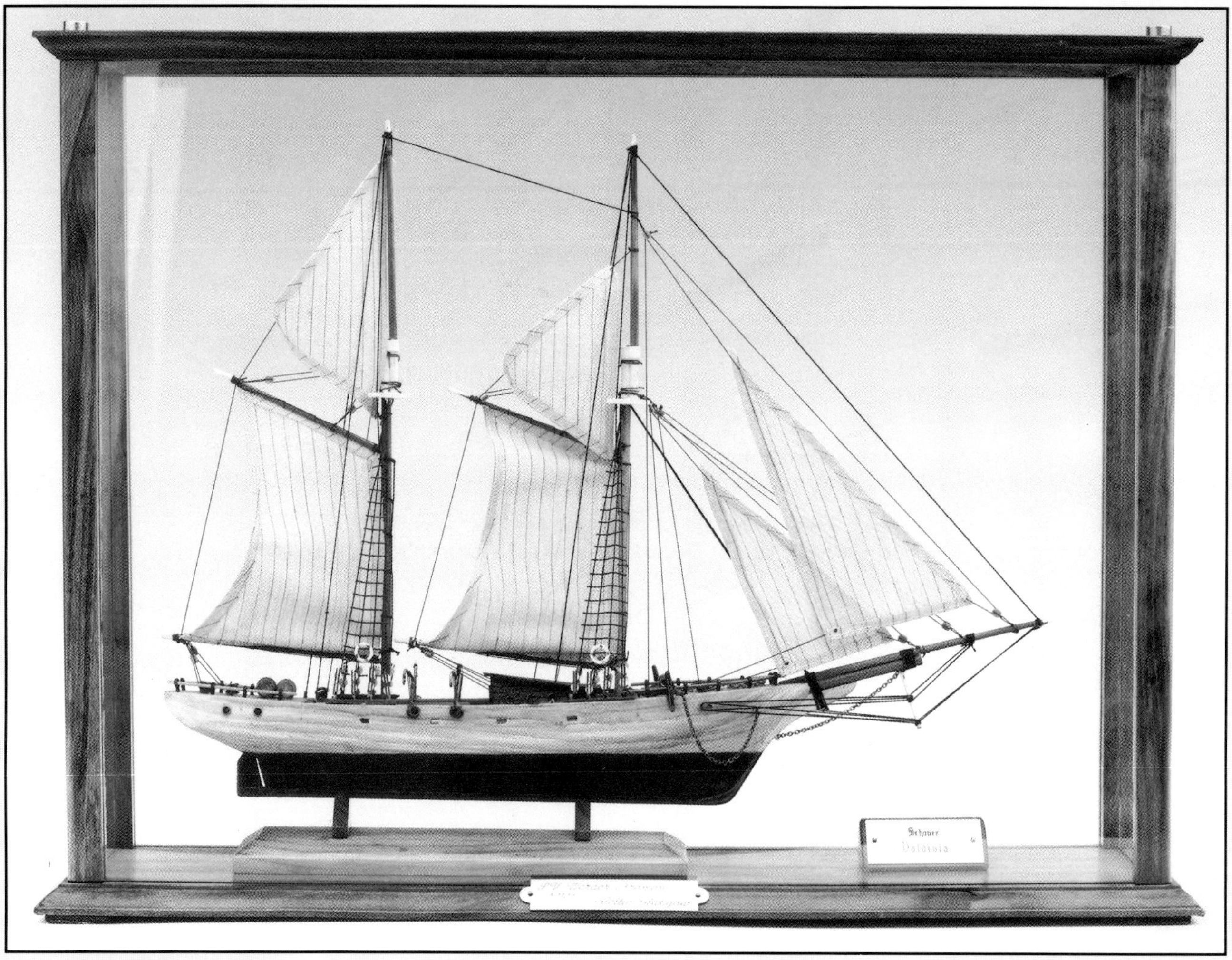

SCHOONER VALDIVIA
1988

Celtic's Centenary champions of 1987/88 were drawn against the German Bundesliga champions in the second round of the following season's European Cup. The right to oppose Werder Bremen was the reward for a good first round 4-1 aggregate win over Honved of Hungary.

In the first leg in Glasgow, the Germans successfully absorbed incessant Celtic pressure and to make matters worse, sneaked a vital away goal in one of their few forays upfield. The return a fortnight later ended goalless after a similar pattern of all-out Celtic attack.

Werder Bremen thus proceeded to the quarter-finals on the strength of their successful guerrilla strike at Parkhead, leaving Celtic with only this wonderful replica sailing ship as consolation.

October 26th: **First Leg**   Celtic 0   Werder Bremen 1

Celtic: Bonner, Morris, Rogan, Aitken, McCarthy, Whyte, Stark (Burns), McStay, McAvennie, McGhee (Walker), Miller.

November 8th: **Second Leg**   Werder Bremen 0   Celtic 0

Celtic: Bonner, Morris, Rogan, Aitken, McCarthy, Whyte, Stark, McStay, McAvennie, McGhee (Archdeacon), Burns (Miller).

Cabinet Size: 21" x 16"

FLEMISH WARRIOR
1984

Dressed and ready for battle, the warrior depicted in this statuette presents a daunting prospect to any would-be aggressor. Perhaps K.A.A. Ghent of Belgium hoped it might intimidate Celtic for the second leg of their first round Cup Winners' Cup encounter of 1984/85.

Ghent held a 1-0 advantage from their home leg, in which they seemed to be making little impression on a disciplined Celtic team until they grabbed the only goal of the match with just nine minutes remaining. The Belgians actually performed well in Glasgow, giving a better account of themselves than the 3-0 scoreline suggests.

The Celtic support could not relax until Paul McStay headed home a minute from time to seal the tie on a 3-1 aggregate.

September 19th: **First Leg**   K.A.A. Ghent 1   Celtic 0

Celtic: Bonner; McGrain, Reid; Aitken, McAdam, MacLeod; Grant, McStay, McClair, Burns, McGarvey.

October 3rd: **Second Leg**   Celtic 3   K.A.A. Ghent 0
McGarvey (40, 61)
McStay (89)

Celtic: Bonner; McGrain, MacLeod; Aitken, McAdam, Grant; Colquhoun (Provan), McStay, McClair, Burns, McGarvey.

Height: 12½"

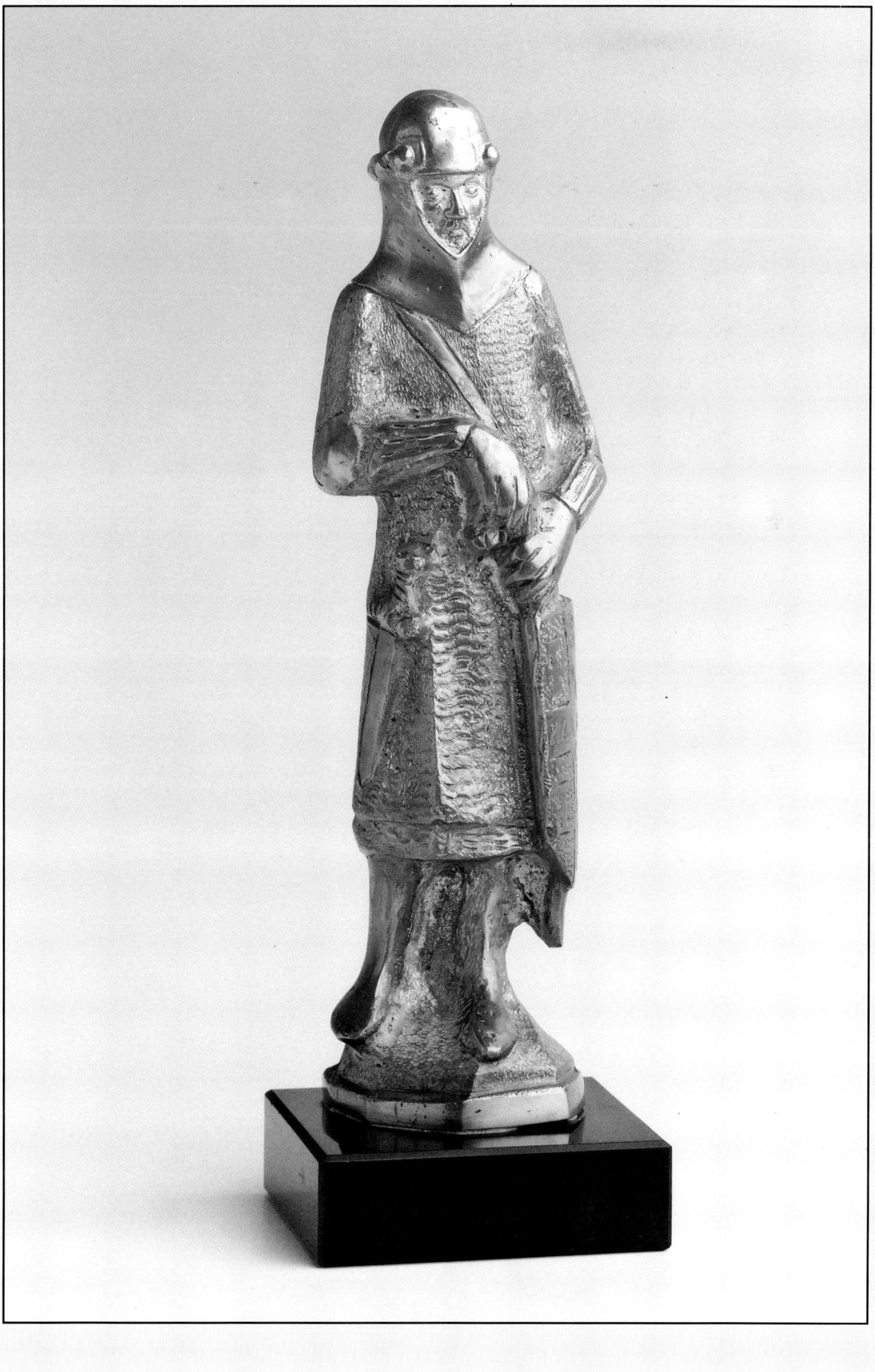

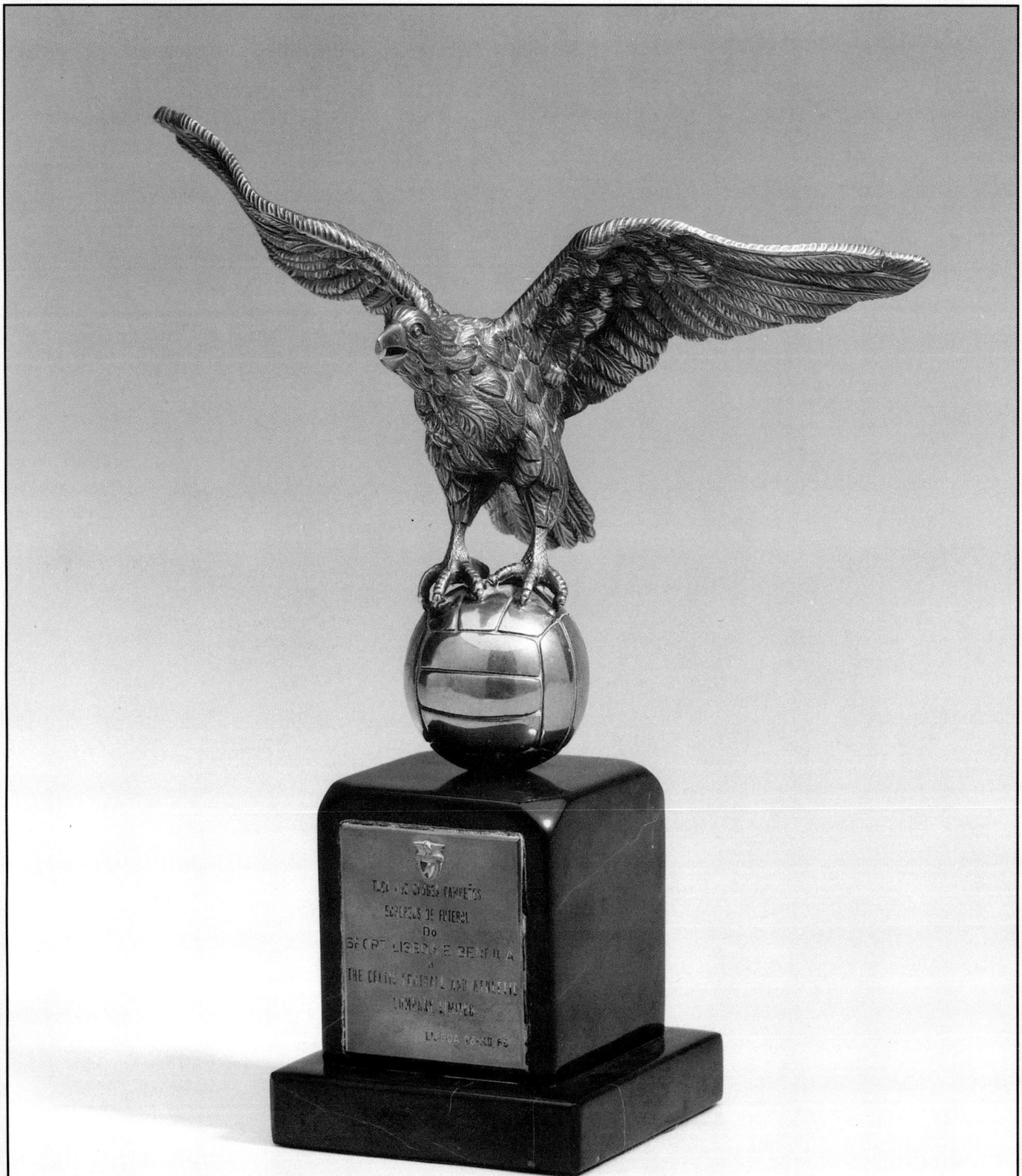

BENFICA EAGLE
1969

Twice European Champions, Benfica of Portugal have as their club crest an eagle perched on a football, poised and ready for take-off. This beautiful replica of that crest was presented to Celtic when the two former winners clashed in the second round of the Champions' Cup of season 1969/70.

Celtic won 3-0 at home in the first leg, though the devastating performance that night really merited a much more convincing victory. Benfica were so overwhelmed that they withdrew strikers Eusebio and Diamentino to switch to a defensive formation in a vain attempt to stem the green and white tide.

The tables were turned two weeks later in Lisbon when Celtic conceded two disastrous goals inside four minutes in the run-up to the interval. The Parkhead men seemed set to survive a backs-to-the-wall second half until Diamentino struck a third two minutes into injury time.

The aggregate score remained level at 3-3 after extra time and Celtic progressed on the toss of a coin, probably an even more nail-biting way of deciding a tie than today's penalty shoot-out, which had not yet been introduced to the European Cup.

November 12th: **First Leg** Celtic 3 Benfica 0
Gemmell (2)
Wallace (41)
Hood (69)

Celtic: Fallon; Craig, Gemmell; Murdoch, McNeill, Clark; Johnstone, Hood, Wallace, Auld, Hughes.

November 26th: **Second Leg** Benfica 3 Celtic 0

Celtic: Fallon; Craig, Gemmell; Murdoch, McNeill, Brogan; Johnstone, Callaghan (Hood), Wallace, Auld (Connelly), Hughes.

Height: 9½"

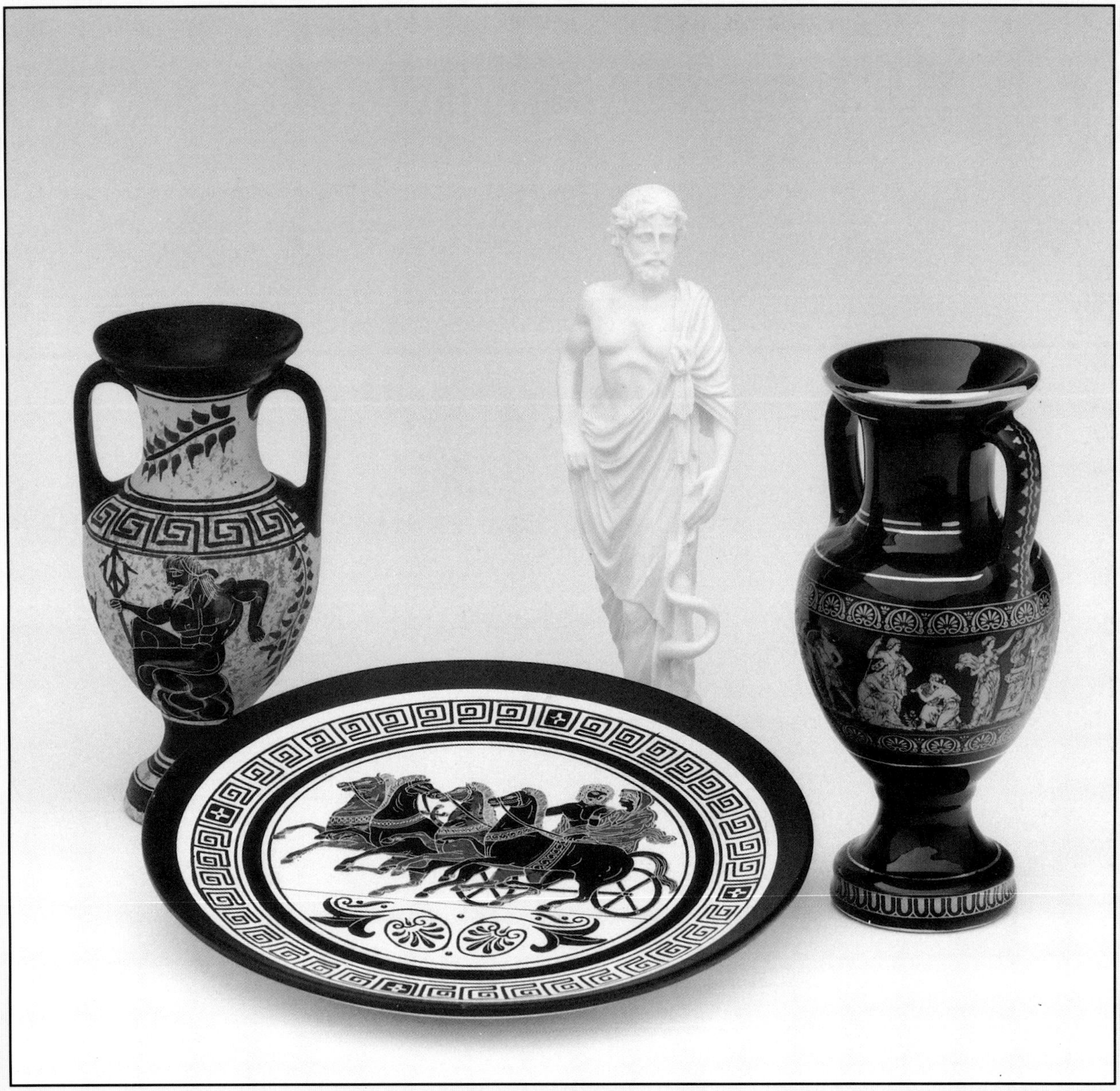

GREEK GIFTS
1974

This handsome selection of items, figurine, vases and plate, was the gift of Olympiakos Piraeus to mark the first round meeting in the European Cup of season 1974/75.

Celtic's first confrontation of Greek opposition had an unhappy outcome with a 3-1 aggregate defeat after only managing a disappointing 1-1 first leg draw at Celtic Park.

September 18th: **First Leg** Celtic 1   Olympiakos 1
Wilson (81)

Celtic: Connaghan; McGrain, Brogan (Lennox); Murray, McNeill, McCluskey; Johnstone, Hood, Dalglish, Callaghan, Wilson.

October 2nd: **Second Leg** Olympiakos 2   Celtic 0

Celtic: Connaghan; McGrain, Brogan; Murray, McNeill, McCluskey; Johnstone (Lennox), Dalglish (Hood), Deans, Callaghan, Wilson.

REAL MADRID GOLDEN BALL
1967

A more typical Real Madrid gift, the golden mounted ball, so curiously symbolic of the señors' erstwhile world football dominance, brings to mind wonderful memories of the dazzling era in which Celtic themselves were masters of all they surveyed in Europe.

On June 7th 1967, fresh from their pinnacle of achievement in the European Cup Final, the 'Lisbon Lions' entered the cauldron of the Santiago Bernabeu Stadium in Madrid to have their new stature tested in the fiercest of fires. Real threw everything at Celtic in an attempt to re-assert themselves in a 'friendly' against their immediate successors as European Champions but the flowering Parkhead maturity prevailed for a 1-0 victory, courtesy of an inspired performance by goalkeeper John Fallon, the solitary strike of 'Buzz-Bomb' Bobby Lennox and a scintillating display by Jimmy Johnstone, who received a standing ovation.

This was the icing on the Lisbon cake, at the personal invitation of the great Alfredo di Stefano, who had wanted nothing but the best for his own benefit match, which this game was.

The Celtic team that day was: Fallon; Craig, Gemmell; Clark, McNeill, O'Neill; Johnstone, Murdoch, Wallace, Auld, Lennox.

Height: 10½"

EL REAL MADRID C.F. AL CELTIC FOOTBALL CLUB
Homenaje a Alfredo Di Stefano
7-VI-1967

VINTAGE MEDALS

This selection of vintage medals and badges is housed in a case contained within the main trophy cabinet in the Celtic Park Board Room. Prominent amongst them are those won by such legendary Celtic figures as Willie Maley, Patsy Gallacher, Jimmy Quinn, Jimmy McMenemy, Charlie Tully and Dan Doyle.

Cabinet Size: 17 1/2" x 28 1/2"

— 101 —

CHARLES PATRICK TULLY
1924 - 1971

NATIONAL HONOURS

LEAGUE CHAMPIONSHIP	1953 - 1954
SCOTTISH CUP	1951 and 1954
SCOTTISH LEAGUE CUP	1956 and 1957
CORONATION CUP	1953
ST. MUNGO'S CUP	1951

INTERNATIONAL HONOURS

NORTHERN IRELAND

VERSUS ENGLAND
1948
1949
1952
1955
VERSUS SCOTLAND
1951
1952
1953
VERSUS WALES
1953
VERSUS FRANCE
1952
VERSUS SPAIN
1958

CHARLES PATRICK TULLY
1948-1959

Charlie Tully will always be remembered as the 'Clown Prince' of Scottish football.

When he landed at the Broomielaw from his native Belfast, Charlie found Celtic at an all-time low ebb. Coming off probably its worst-ever season, in which unthinkable relegation was only narrowly avoided, the club and its long-suffering support were never more in need of a hero. Tully was that with a vengeance, as his on-field antics and irrepressible personality sustained Celtic throughout a period which, though not spectacularly successful, encompassed several 'landmark' achievements.

The austere 'fifties brought Celtic The St Mungo Cup (1951), The Coronation Cup (1953) and the club's first 'double' for decades (1953/54). In addition there were two Scottish Cups and two League Cups, including the club's single most celebrated domestic result, the immortal '7-1' defeat of Rangers in the 1957 final.

'Cheeky Charlie' was a major influence in all of these triumphs and along the way purveyed immense pleasure to the footballing public at large and the Celtic 'faithful' in particular.

With a twinkle in his eye and a jaunty stride, Charlie was the undisputed darling of Celtic Park throughout a historic decade.

His memorial cabinet is here enhanced by a personal emerald cygnet ring.

Cabinet Size: 23¾" x 22½"

CENTENARY GIFTS
1988

Below and opposite is a representative selection of the mementoes showered on Celtic to commemorate a hundred glorious years:

SILVER SALVER *from the Scottish Football Association.*

SILVER CIGARETTE BOX *from the Scottish League.*

MARE & FOAL STATUETTE *from Motherwell F.C., illustrative of the many beautiful gifts from other clubs.*

CENTENARY SCULPTURE *from the Celtic Supporters' Association.*

CELTIC
CENTENARY 1888-1988
The Celtic Supporters Association

THIS JERSEY WAS WORN BY JOHNNY CRUM
IN THE EXHIBITION CUP FINAL OF 1938
JOHNNY SCORED THE WINNING GOAL IN
THE 1-0 DEFEAT OF EVERTON.

JOHNNY CRUM'S JERSEY
1938

While perhaps lacking a little in the modern 'designer' stakes, this exhibit is perennially fashionable with the Celtic set. Being the actual jersey worn by the scorer of the winning goal of the Empire Exhibition Final (see page 80), it forms, together with the match ball and the trophy itself, a priceless hat-trick of souvenirs of an occasion which is one of the beacons of Celtic history.

The precious artefacts match the trio of goals notched by centre-forward Crum in disposing of Sunderland, Hearts and Everton within the week of the tournament.

Though threadbare in places, this relic and the rich memories it evokes remain brand new for anyone with a sense of Celtic tradition and lore.

Cabinet Size: 20" x 25"

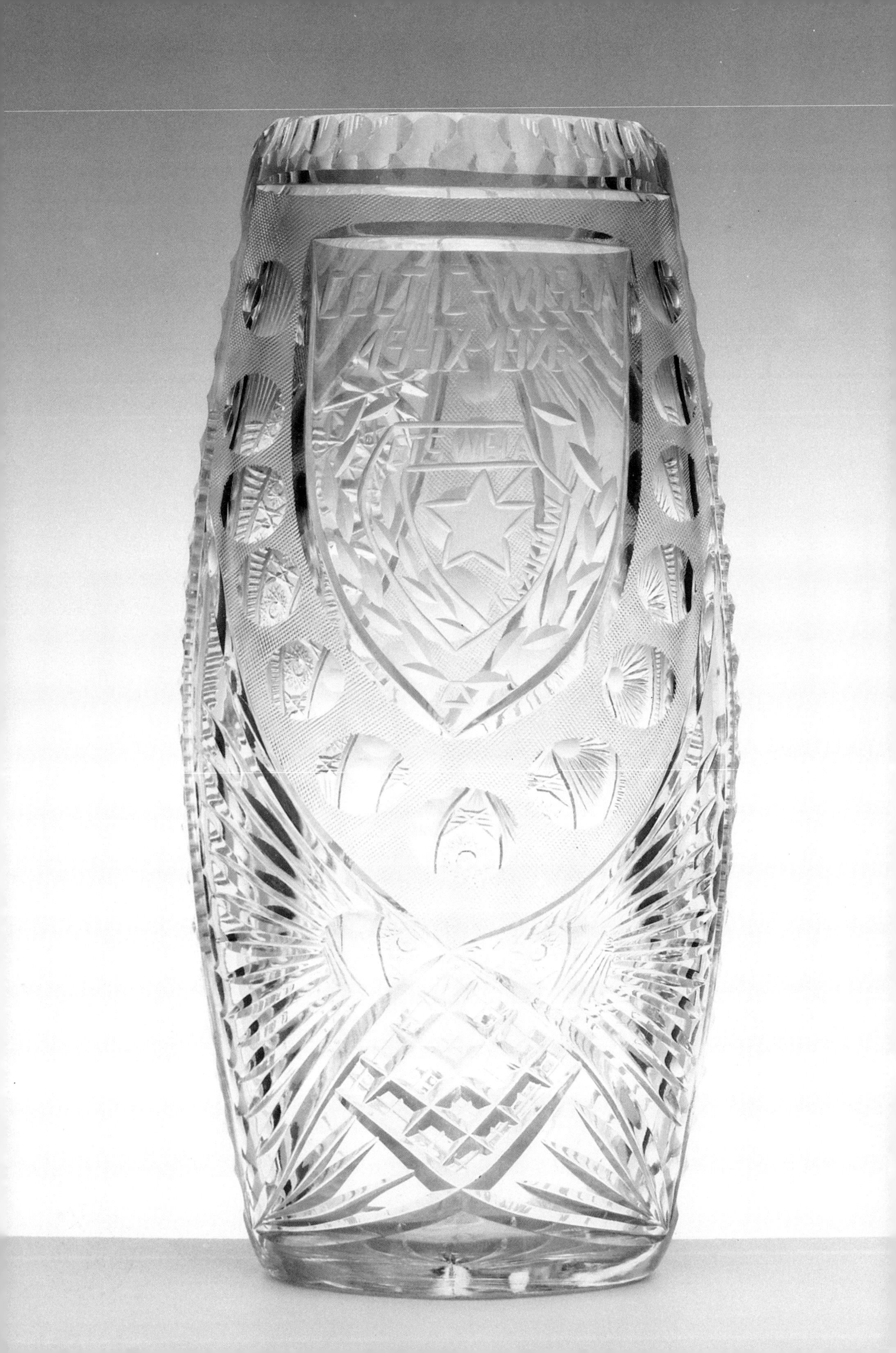

KRAKOW VASE
1976

Season 1976/77 was a bittersweet one for Celtic. Though it ended triumphantly in a League and Cup 'double' with a 1-0 victory over Rangers at Hampden on May 7th, chances of the elusive 'treble' had slipped away with the frustrating loss of the League Cup final to Aberdeen the previous November.

That hiccup had been the low point of a 'stop-go' sticky patch which encompassed the onset of the U.E.F.A. Cup campaign. Celtic were paired in the first round with Wisla Krakow, opponents who typified the traditional Polish blend of skill and toughness. Despite the promise of a thirteenth minute strike by Roddie MacDonald, the home first leg gradually went sour and only a last-gasp Dalglish equalizer kept faint hopes flickering for the return in Poland.

Two stunning goals within five second half minutes in Krakow by Wisla's World Cup striker Kmiecik settled the tie on a 4-2 aggregate to conclude the season's brief European episode for Celtic.

Stylish compensation for an 'early bath' came in the shape of this handsomely engraved vase.

September 15th: **First Leg** Celtic 2 Wisla Krakow 2
MacDonald (13)
Dalglish (90)

Celtic: Latchford; McGrain, Lynch; Glavin, MacDonald, Edvaldsson; Doyle, Dalglish, Wilson, Burns, Lennox.

September 29th: **Second Leg** Wisla Krakow 2 Celtic 0

Celtic: Latchford; McGrain, Lynch; McCluskey, Edvaldsson, MacDonald; Glavin, Aitken, Doyle (Lennox), Dalglish, Wilson.

Height: 11½"

Presented To GLASGOW CELTIC F.C.
By The People Of Ballymote On The
Official Opening Of
Brother WALFRID KERINS Memorial Park
5th June 1989

BROTHER WALFRID MEMORIAL BOWL
1989

A club delegation led by the then Chairman, Jack McGinn, travelled to Ballymote in Ireland's County Sligo for the official opening on June 5th 1989 of the Brother Walfrid Kerins Memorial Park, a new football ground dedicated to the memory of The Celtic Football Club's principal founding father. The Celtic party presented a Brother Walfrid portrait to hang in his home town pavilion and accepted this magnificent crystal bowl in return from the townspeople of Ballymote.

The bowl has been given a place of suitable pre-eminence within Celtic Park, as befits any memento of such a major figure in the club's history.

Another giant in Celtic history, the legendary Willie Maley, whose connection with the club stretched back to the very earliest days, reflecting on Brother Walfrid's death in the Annual Report of June 1st, 1915, depicted him as 'the last of the leading founders of the Celtic club . . . (who) . . . must have spent a considerable period near the blarney stone in his young days, as his persuasive powers, once experienced, could never be forgotten'.

Celtic people the world over rejoice in the legacy of this remarkable man.

Height: 19 3/4"

ACKNOWLEDGEMENTS

The authors and publishers are immensely grateful to John C. McGinn, Director and former Chairman of The Celtic Football Club, without whose co-operation and assistance their task might never have been accomplished.

Sincere thanks also go to Donald Cowey, editor of 'The Celtic View' and to The Celtic Football Club itself.

Domestic Trophies

Celtic have, of course, been consistent winners of the three major domestic competitions, the League Championship, the Scottish Cup and the League Cup. However, as their possession is periodic and non-exclusive, they are not included in this volume.

NOTES ON TEXT

All measurements are approximate.

Goal timings have been omitted in a few cases where either the information was not available or space did not alllow.

All facts and figures are correct as far as could be ascertained at time of printing.